ANALYZING THE NOVEL

**Dragonslaying
is for
Dreamers**

National Writing Institute
810 Damon Ct.
Houston TX 77006-1329

Manufactured in the United States of America

ISBN 1888344-27-X

For information on discounts for classroom sets or for institutional use, write National Writing Institute, 810 Damon Ct., Houston, TX 77006-1329

INTRODUCTION

Reading is one of the most important things that young people can do. But, just to read a great deal is not enough. Young people need to discuss the ideas they experience. They need to talk to adults about the values they find expressed by the heroes of their books. Mortimer Adler, a philosophy professor at the University of Chicago for forty years, and author of *How to Read a Book* and the creator of the great books discussion techniques, said in a speech given at Kalamazoo College when he was 92 years old: "If our culture is saved, it must be done by our children—it's too late for us to do it. They can save it only if they have internalized the values of our culture. To do this they must identify with our cultural heroes. Not the rock and sports stars, but the heroes of our great literature. To do this identification, they must discuss the ideas in the literature they read with adults. We must discuss these ideas with our children."

What Adler asks of us is not an easy thing to do. I taught bright seniors for years before I was comfortable with the discussion of ideas generated by fiction. A discussion, to do the most good, must be organized, therefore the structure of fiction must be understood. That's the purpose of this manual for adults. It's designed to give you help when you teach the elements of novels. The analysis here is based on the book *Dragonslaying Is For Dreamers* and is intended to serve as an example or model of how to examine any novel. It shows you how to take this one book apart, so that when your students have read it, they can benefit from any directed discussions about this and consequently any novel they read.

There are invented conversations with a bright twelve-year-old and with a class of students to demonstrate how children can be led to understand the elements of fiction. Even if you've taken courses in novel examination, this book will make your task of training young minds in that exercise easier. This is not a program or a lesson plan. It's intended to be a resource book for the teacher. It would be best to read it in one sitting and then to refer to it as you and your students work your way through *Dragonslaying is for Dreamers* and then use the ideas contained here for the discussion of any fiction.

CONTENTS

OVERVIEW

Dragonslaying is for Dreamers is a fantasy novel. This means that the laws of nature, as we know them, may be violated. Once the reader accepts a story as fantasy, the violations encountered must also be accepted. In some fantasies rabbits can talk, in others there may be giants and very small people, or whole worlds underground or in the clouds, or it might be possible for horses to fly. These violations allow the writer to deal with the ideas in the fiction is such a way that they can be abstracted and examined by the readers as the characters experience them.

This book, which takes place in a period that is not real—it has never happened—has dragons in it. There is no suggestion that at one time there were dragons that knights fought with for honor and treasure. They are used by this author to create an adventure for the young hero. They give him a target and a way to fulfill his goals. They are used by the author as an antagonistic force. As such, they must be shown to be very powerful, and the hero must destroy them to realize his dream.

As in all novels, the hero in this one, Axel, must overcome great odds to be successful. The dragons he must kill for the bounty represent or are symbols for, at least for the reader, a much larger force—the elements of his culture and the circumstances of his life that make it hard for him to attain the status and assume the responsibilities of manhood.

You will recognize that the young hero has been created so as to make it easy for young readers to identify with him. He then is given a problem he must solve in order to marry a girl he loves and to be able to support them both by farming.

There are a number of sub-plots in this story which are intended to create suspense and give color to the lives of the hero and the girl he loves.

The examination of this novel is divided by both chapters and structural elements. There are no lesson plans here, rather there is background and explanation for you as teacher. You'll have to determine the types of discussions and the topics covered based on the age and experience of your students.

There is little value for students to be given tests on the books they read that ask them to recall information given in the text. That is the lowest form of intellectual experience. Nor, is there benefit for students to tell the story in their own words. This is often done, but the story was well told once by the author and to ask young readers to try and tell it again is an insult both to the story and the student.

This book is an examination of the structure of an adventure/fantasy novel. Use it to help you guide your students to an understanding of any story or novel. It was written to help you *discuss* this book *with* young readers. It is not a guide for lectures or tests. The presenting of the values of reading to young people is best realized in talking with them. These talks should not be conducted as a test with right and wrong answers. This puts pressure on the students, and it gets in the way of them exploring freely the ideas in the fiction. It would help both you and your students if you made it clear to them that you will never tell them that the ideas that they get from their reading are wrong. This is a common practice in schools and it greatly inhibits free discussion. After all, we ask the students to tell us what they think, and when they do, we must not indicate to them that their thinking is poor or wrong.

Every time you ask your students to tell you what they think, their answers must be given respect. This means that you can't say, "Okay, anyone else?" and then seize on the next answer as the correct one. When students tell you what they think, you're given a gift of their thoughts. Treat their ideas as gifts, even if you don't like or agree with them. While discussing literature, it isn't a bad idea to start with the understanding that there may be no "right" answers to questions concerning what students think or feel. This is hard to get used to, because we, as educated adults, know so much more than our students and have good reasons for thinking as we do. But keep in mind, as your students are learning to love literature, that you're not asking them to memorize facts or to assume a body of knowledge but to recognize their intellectual and emotional responses and to make attempts to understand what causes them.

Chapter 1

There Are Two Kinds Of Falling

In which we are introduced to the hero and his problem. We see his village, his friend, and how he is handling the death of his father.

When you introduce this book, you might point out to your students that in many books chapter headings can help with understanding. In the case of chapter one, the meaning is very clear. Axel starts to fall from a cliff, and he begins to fall for a girl, Molly. Your students will catch this on their own, but you might bring their attention to it anyway.

Many of these chapter titles have a sports reference, or are things coaches say to their players. Since this novel is what is called a "rites of passage" novel, these references to sports give the sub-titles an ironic flavor, at least for young American readers, for involvement in sports is one of the very few ways our society has provided as a means of passage into manhood for boys. The use of sports as a rite of passage is seen by some as a destructive influence. That might make a good discussion topic.

SETTING

Setting is the term used for the time period and location of fiction. In books written for small children, this is often spelled out clearly. In novels for young adults, the readers usually are sophisticated enough that the indicators of time and location can be suggested by description and dialogue.

LOCATION:

Establishing location almost always occurs in the first chapter. Look at page 1: *Large stones projected from the first grass covering the ground as it fell quickly to the river.* This tells readers that there are seasons, and that they are severe enough to kill off the grass in winter. This story then must take place in a temperate or a colder climate. . . . *heavy and full with the spring run off.* This indicates snow or ice melting. This only occurs where the temperature is cold enough so that snow can accumulate—either in a northern temperate zone or in the mountains. So, in just three lines, we have learned to place the action in the mountains or above a zone that would include the latitude, in this country, that is described as the rust belt. We also know by now that the characters here are not in a desert or in the tropics.

Notice that when I talk about the events of this book, I use present tense—as if those actions were taking place as I speak about them. Even when talking about characters, present tense should be used. This doesn't make sense in any logical way but it's the way it's done. It will help your students if you insist that they do likewise. It might seem awkward for them at first, but they'll soon get used to it.

On page 1:. . . *the few small houses of Greenwater lay scattered. . .* tells us that the location for the opening action may be a small village.

On page 2: . . . *wound the hole made in ground at the side of the temple. . .* we learn that the father is buried in the yard of a temple, not a common practice in the cities in this country.

On page 2: . . . *and recognize the plowsmell of fresh soil. . .* we learn by the character's remembrance of the smell of the fresh dirt of his father's grave as "plowsmell," that this character is familiar with the smells of farming. Axel is placed on a farm on page 5 where he thinks: *I can work the farm as good as my father did. . .almost.*

TIME:

On page 1:. . . *the first grass of the year*, we learn it is spring. This is obvious to us, but it might be good to point out that the clues are there and it is important to recognize them as that.

On page 4: . . . *winding, narrow track to the village,. . .* and, later on the same page . . . *walking in the mud-rutted and wet dirt.*

Page 5: . . . *he looked quickly at her then back at the road.* These three passages tell us that the road to the village is still a "track." This gives an indication of the time of the novel. It is before there were paved roads such as we know them. Still, it is after the use of some machinery, the kind that would leave tracks and would need a road.

Page 5:. . . *really sick, and there was so much pain, and he could hear him moaning in his bed, even when he was outside doing the chores,* tells us that the time of this novel is either before pain relievers (morphine etc) or there will be some compelling reason why the family would let the father die in great pain.

Page 6: . . . *she'll want her jug of ale,* gives us a good clue. We haven't purchased beer or ale in jugs or pails in the last 80 years. This means that in this world, or time, or place, they don't do things like we do them now.

CHARACTERS

The characters in novels are central to everything else the writers deal with. All good literature examines what is called the human condition. This is often referred to by the label of universal themes, and deals with a person's relationships with other people, parents or children, societies and institutions, governing bodies, self awareness, laws, natural forces, and the significance of life and death. This means that a bright, perceptive artist has looked at what it means to be human and alive and writes into his fiction what he understands about people and their problems, anxieties and relationships. These observations deal with major ideas such as:

1. Religion and how it guides people's lives and helps or hinders them in making decisions
2. Death and its nature or consequences
3. Love and what it means to people and the things it allows them to do and experience
4. Society and its benefits and restrictions
5. Responsibility and the decisions it imposes
6. Laws and concepts of justice
7. Freedom and the necessity to make the choices it demands
8. Control: who has it and over whom and how it is resisted
9. Growth, both as individuals and as groups of people
10. The non-statutory rules that guide behavior and how they are circumvented or followed and the consequences of either choice
11. Work, what it produces and what it gives to individuals involved or takes from life
12. Parent/child and man/woman relationships

When a writer gives us an understanding of some aspect of the human condition, he or she must do so in the context of a story, because that's the nature of fiction. All novels have characters. These "people" are very carefully created to fill a complicated function.

Before creating the characters of a novel, a writer makes many decisions. These have to do with the writer's understanding of the effect the characteristics and actions of the characters will have on the selected readership. Some of the major ones are about the following:

1. The age, intelligence, reading level, sex, interest, and ethnic and cultural background of the intended readership
2. The nature of the conflict
3. The forces in conflict
4. The part each character must play in that conflict. (This determines the motivations and limitations of the characters.)
5. The relationships the characters have with each other and how this influences their roles in the conflict

CHARACTER IDENTIFICATION

Character identification is the process of readers reacting to characters in a positive way. This reaction is carefully orchestrated by good writers. If readers do not identify with the main characters in fiction, they can't empathize with the characters and the predicaments and joys the characters experience. Thus the identification process is essential. The three methods by which a writer can encourage this process of identification are by:

1. Creating a character who is very similar to the intended readership so that the readers will recognize that they are like the character
2. Creating a character who the intended readership would like to be like
3. Creating a character who the readers know so much about that they understand why the character acts and reacts as he or she does

This process works this way: If I'm a writer and my intended readership is nine or ten year-old girls, I'd create a character who would be about 12 or 13 years old. My readers would find it easy to identify with a girl three or four years older than they are. Most nine year old girls would like to be like and to do the things a 12 or 13 year-old does.

This need for the identification process produces this situation: Scary books are read and enjoyed by girls in their early teens. The main characters are high school age. Adventure books are read by boys between 10 and 18. The characters are young adults. Horse books are enjoyed by young girls about 10 to 13 years old and the major characters are usually 13 to 18 years old. I, in my late middle age, am not interested in horse books, as a young person would not be interested in a story about a retired teacher and the problems that person might have.

On page 1 we learn that the main character is named *Axel* and is a person who many of the intended readership would see themselves to be similar to, and would also like to be like. This is not a common name for middle class American readers. In fact, except for one movie, I've never run into the name before. But it does have an Anglo Saxon ring to it. It is not like Blademire or Gordo, or Vincenti. This is a name that most young male readers in the U.S. could easily identify with.

In the first ten lines, we learn that Axel lives in a climate much like the one where most of us live. This creates a reaction in us that is much different than the one we might have if the description were of a desert or of a frozen landscape like the one that could be found in Siberia or northern Alaska.

On page 1 we learn that Axel is alone and in pain. . . . *through tears he couldn't stop.* Most young readers could easily identify with being alone when they cry and are feeling badly. This is one of the common constant conditions of adolescence. On page 2 we learn the reason for the tears. The worry about the death of a parent is something that most teenagers experience. Children, until the age of about 11 or 12 see their parents as always there and their permanence is a given, but about then they understand that life is temporary, and the problem that Axel faces becomes a real possibility for them. It is easy for them to identify with this situation and then with Axel.

Page 2:   *. . .desperate ache of his wanting to be with his father, wherever that was, to follow him and be near him again. Imagining for the last two days what it would be like living alone with his mother had left him in doubt that he could do it.*

We know that Axel has lost his father but we also understand that for some reason he doesn't want to continue to live with his mother. By this time your students should begin to recognize this process that this author is putting them through.

Page 3:   *. . .Axel hadn't cried for years, and he wouldn't allow himself to at the funeral, but now he couldn't stop. It was as if there were a hole in his chest, filled to bursting, and the only way he could get out the air was by sobbing. Molly held him as his body shuddered.*

Axel, like our readers, resists crying in public—or even at all—and the one he feels most comfortable with is another person of his age.

Page 3:   *". . .I've been worried about you ever since your father got sick. When I saw you up here standing on the edge of that stone and looking down, I didn't know what you were thinking. Are you sure you're going to be all right?"*

Axel's friend, Molly, is understanding, compassionate, and is worried about him. The reader should like such a person, and would be likely to identify with a character who this kind person would care about.

Page 4:   *. . .Axel had never had a conversation like this with anyone before. No one had ever asked him how he felt or if he would be all right. It was strange, but good.*

Axel, like most young people, hasn't had a conversational relationship with adults. We could expect the reader to feel this way. Very few of the students I've worked with in my 30 years of teaching had had conversations with adults in which they were asked how they felt about important things. Most young readers should identify with Axel on this point. In the rest of the chapter, the reader sees Axel experience what most young people do at the emergence of their relationships with others.

In this first chapter, the young reader is presented with a character carefully designed to be easily identified with. Axel lives in a small town in a part of the world much like the readers'. He's just a few years older than the expected readers, has lost a parent and is in great pain because of it. Axel has some of the same experiences that most of the readers understand because they are experiencing the same ones in their relationships with other young people.

This process of identification is important if readers are to empathize with Axel. Of course Axel will face great dangers, and if the readers don't identify with him, then they won't empathize with (feel for) him. Without this condition there can be no suspense or drama to any story.

CONFLICT

Conflict in novels is the struggle characters have with forces. This struggle can be with other characters, situations or the natural forces of nature, like wind, as in *Twister* or fire as in *Flashback* or animals as in *Shark* or *Grizzly,* or with governments as in *Hunt for Red October,* or situations as in *Airport*, or in relationships as in *The Bridges of Madison County.* Whatever it is, it is essential in fiction that these conflicts be resolved. Without conflict and its resolution, there can be no traditional story. Some post-modern fiction is constructed differently, but your students won't need to know about that for years yet. These conflicts are usually referred to by the following labels:
1. **person against person**
2. **person against nature**
3. **person against society**
4. **person against self**

In these forms:

1. **Person against person** is a conflict where two people want the same thing, and the conflict (struggle) is over which one will get it. One person may want to do or get something and the other person makes this difficult. This form of conflict can develop between best friends, a husband and wife, a boss and a worker, two people at opposite sides of some issue or special interest (such as cowboys and sheep herders) and can center on objects such as a bike, a tree house, an oil field or country, or it could be over an intangible thing like an idea.

2. **Person against nature** is a conflict where one character (it could even be a group) has a struggle with the elements of nature. It might be to survive a storm, to fly a plane, climb a mountain, have a picnic on a rainy day, create an ice skating rink when there is no water, find a honey tree, or any of hundreds of other situations in which characters might find themselves.

3. **Person against society** is a conflict where one character is in a struggle with a group to which that member belongs. This could be a person who does not want to do what the group thinks is best or right to do. This character might not want to rob a bank, allow for the building of a toxic waste dump in the county, go to war or pick on an unfortunate neighbor.

4. **Person against self** is a conflict between two forces within a character. This could be with the body's desire to eat more than it should and the knowledge that this is not a good thing to do, a desire to have something even if it means to steal it and the knowledge that stealing is wrong, a feeling of guilt over something that has been done, a fear of doing something that has to be done, or any situation where a character must or must not do something.

The sides of the conflict and the characteristics of the elements which are in conflict are understood as the protagonist and the antagonist forces:

1. **Protagonist forces** or characters are those which want something. This is remembered because the word starts with *pro*. The hero or the main character is usually on this side of the conflict.

2. **Antagonist forces** or characters are those which are against or want to stop the protagonist from succeeding. This is remembered because the word starts with *ant* (a variation of the prefix *anti*). This is usually the side of the conflict which has the "evil" person or the bad force, like bad weather or greed.

The strengths of the two sides must be equal or must differ in prescribed ways, for, if there were to be a conflict between a powerful protagonist force and a weak antagonist force, there would be no contest and the conflict would not create suspense. As an example, if a professional football team (the protagonist force) were to have a game with a team from a local high school (the antagonist force), this would not be much of a conflict, and the watcher (reader) would not worry about the "good" professional team being beaten.

On the other hand, if a high school football team were to be the protagonist force and were to be pitted against a team of superior ability (the antagonist), there could be much suspense. This is why the heroes in adventure stories are very often alone or do not have strong forces to help them. They must overcome great odds and trick or outwit very powerful "evil" forces or characters to be successful or to get what they want.

The nature of the forces created will determine the type of conflict that takes place.

1. If the conflict is an **internal** one (one that takes place within a character, such as with a desired act and a guilty conscience), then, for the reader to make sense of the story, this aspect of this character must be understood. The writer must help the reader focus on this

9

character and what the character's desires are (the protagonist force) and what there is about the other force (the opposing antagonist force) that is trying to keep those desires from being satisfied.

2. If the conflict is an **external** one (one that is between a character and some outside force, such as nature) then, for the reader to make sense of the story, these two forces—the character and the outside force—must be understood. The reader must be helped to focus on these two forces as the external antagonist force tries to defeat the desires of the protagonist character. This is the type of conflict that Axel faces.

As you and your students work with literature, you'll find the following types of conflicts. It might be good to introduce them to your students in advance. They won't help you with this novel, but this would give your students an introduction to them.

PERSON AGAINST PERSON:

In many stories the conflict is between two of the main characters. In this type of conflict the two forces are represented by people. These characters—whether individuals or groups are pitted against each other. The conflict of the novel is resolved when one group or person is successful.

PERSON AGAINST NATURE:

Many adventure stories are written with the major conflict between a person and some element of nature. This might be the ocean, the cold of winter, a storm, flood, fire or wind. The story of man's struggle against these large natural forces is fascinating to many people. In this case in this book, the natural force is the dragon.

In order for this type of conflict to be meaningful, the nature of the natural force must be understood. Many writers assume that their readers will understand conditions such as hypothermia or dehydration or how easy it is to become disoriented in a woods, but if the characteristics of the natural force are not understood and not explained, it will be difficult for some readers to appreciate the story.

PERSON AGAINST SOCIETY:

A very popular conflict is with a person against a group of people who are in control. Often this group is called society and it may be represented by school teachers and administrators, city government workers, neighborhood council members, church leadership, members of a club or organization or a government or governmental agency. The writer must help the reader to understand the dynamics of the group and the power groups have.

Axel in this novel must fight against the **forces in his society** that prevent him from becoming a man. They are in part:
1. **Economic**
2. **Parental**
3. **Social**
4. **Physical**
5. **Educational**

These are not covered in chapter one, but in this novel Axel battles against not having enough money to marry Molly and support her. He is handicapped by his mother and her weaknesses and the responsibility he feels to care for her. The society has not educated him to be a man, and ridicules his attempts to assert himself as such. He is not fully grown; he is still a slight teenager. He must learn a great deal to be able to make enough money to be independent of his mother and of his town and its restrictions.

PERSON AGAINST SELF:

Some stories are written so that the main characters have what are called internal conflicts. They center on "better judgment" or conscience or moral or religious training. The characters want to do things known to be wrong or have done things and now feel guilty about having done them.

SUB-PLOTS

In many novels, as in this one, there are what are called sub-plots. These, too, have conflicts that must be resolved.

On page 11 we are first introduced to the conflict in this novel. Your readers may not recognize this yet as one aspect of the central conflict, but soon should. The major conflict in this novel is between Axel, the main character, and the forces in society that inhibit his easy transition from childhood to manhood. This then is what is called a rites of passage conflict. In order for your students to understand this novel at this level, the rites of passage may have to be discussed.

In primitive societies there were and are rituals that were and are experienced so that this passage can be smoothly made. For instance, activities such as fasting and the picking out of a name is part of this activity for some American Indians. Some religious experiences help some boys in this. The Jewish religion has a bar mitzvah ceremony, after which the boy is given the responsibilities of his decisions. Some African tribes in the past have had the killing of a lion as part of this passage. This is no longer done and is now replaced with other rituals, among which are dancing and feasting.

This is a fantasy novel, so the conditions that exist for Axel that inhibit his passage may or may not exist as such in contemporary societies. Nevertheless, they exist for Axel, and for him they are real. There will be much more introduction of this conflict in chapter two.

The passage to manhood for young boys, if not accompanied by acts of bravery or ritual, is traumatic for many young men. How do they demonstrate to themselves and others that they have become men and should be considered as such? Many cultures have solved this problem for their young men. Some of the things that we do in this country do help some. In America, the transition to manhood is demonstrated by the boy earning a driver's license, by a job, by the wearing of that first suit and the first formal dance, by organized sports in high school, or by enlistment in the military. But, not having that line between boyhood and manhood clearly defined is a problem for many young men. This is the conflict in this novel for the main character in his world. Axel can't function in his society as a man because there are no methods by which this transition can be accomplished.

He is faced with this problem in the form of not having the means to support a wife and family. There are no programs in his society to help him. He must solve this problem by himself.

One of the sub-plots is also introduced in this first chapter. On page 4: *What will your mother do now, Axel?* gives us another conflict (problem) that must be resolved before the story closes. We learn that Axel's mother also has an uncertain future and that Axel is worried about her and what will happen to her. In chapter two we learn more about this conflict dealing with children's responsibility for their parents.

INCITING FORCE

This is an action or event that triggers the conflict. It doesn't have to be a major move or an important event. Some small thing might set off the conflict, but at this point the character is introduced to the situation that becomes the conflict that can destroy or damage the character.

Axel is presented with the first introduction to the conflict—the inciting force—with his father's death. He is thrust into the position of "man of the house." He must function as an adult and provide for his mother, and he can't, because society has no mechanism for him to become an adult. In his world's eyes, he is still a child. In chapter two we find that there is a conjunction between this sub-plot and its conflict and the main plot conflict.

Page 2:   . . . *he could see the lighter color of the fresh dirt where they had covered his father that afternoon.*

Page 2:   *. . .there was a force that pulled him down. He was drawn by the desperate ache of his wanting to be with his father, wherever that was, to follow him and be near him again. Imagining for last two days what it would be like living alone with his mother, had left him in doubt that he could do it.*

This conflict and the conflict in the sub-plot are of real importance to Axel. We witness what may be an attempt at suicide, or at least the suggestion of its possibility. Molly thinks so, anyway.

Page 4:   *". . .When I saw you up here, standing on the edge of that stone and looking down, I didn't know what you were thinking. Are you sure you're going to be all right?"*

This is reinforced by Molly.

Page 4:   *She held his shirt in both of her hands and shook him lightly and said, "Because, I really worry about what happens to you. You know that, don't you?"*

POINT OF VIEW

Point of view is the name given for the conditions of the narrative voice in fiction. There are many choices authors can make, and these must be understood by readers if fiction is to make sense.

You might want to examine the following chart for the options that an author has in selecting point of view. This has to be a conscious choice on the author's part, for if the point of view shifts, it gets very confusing for the reader.

NARRATIVE VOICE
POINT OF VIEW CHOICES

PERSON: Singular or Plural	First *I* or *we*	Second *you*	Third *she*, *he* or *they*
TENSE:	Past	Present	Future
ATTITUDE:	Objective		Subjective
INVOLVEMENT:	Part of Action		Observer
KNOWLEDGE:	Limited Omniscient		Restricted to Participation
PERSPECTIVE:	Omnipresent Overview		Restricted to Participation

---

In the first sentence of the book, we learn much information about the choices this author makes in the selection of the narrative voice's point of view.

Page 1: *Axel stood on the sharp end of the boulder and could feel the toes of his boots hanging over the edge.*

PERSON & TENSE   Axel stood: **third person singular** and **past tense**.

KNOWLEDGE   *. . . could feel the toes of his boots hanging over the edge.*

limited omniscient (The narrative voice tells us that Axel could feel his toes over the edge. To do this, the voice would have to be in Axel's mind, hence a form of omniscience.)

INVOLVEMENT   **non-involved observer** (The narrative voice sees Axel but isn't involved in him standing there. Axel is alone on the rock.)

Page 2:   *He looked toward the houses, and through tears he couldn't stop, watched smoke from the few chimneys as it rose slowly in thin lines then flattened into a faint haze that followed the course of the river.*

ATTITUDE   **objective** (The narrative voice doesn't tell us how it feels about Axel's pain. For this to be a subjective voice, it would have to read like this: *It was sad to see Axel standing there alone, in the rain, with the tears running down his face.*)

PERSPECTIVE   **restricted to participation**

Page 1:   *From where he stood, he could see the road as it passed his village* (At this point we don't know what is happening outside of Axel's sight or knowledge. The narrative voice is restricted to what Axel can see and know from his position.)

These choices do not change, and in most novels the introduced narrative voice conditions remain constant. It might be valuable for your students to find examples in other novels of different narrative voice conditions and discuss them.

EXPOSITION

Exposition is the giving of information. So that the events of the novel make sense, the reader must be given knowledge, in some way, of the following:

1. The time or period
2. The location
3. The characters'
   A. Ages
   B. Backgrounds
   C. Relationships
   D. Goals (what they want or what they expect to get from each other or from the situation)
   E. The events that have led to the situation at the opening of the novel

This must be done for each new character or condition as it is introduced to the reader. As your students work through this book, you might have them make notes of or relate to you the expository information they recognize at the introduction of each new character and/or event.

As an example of exposition in this novel, it might benefit your students to look at the characters introduced in the first chapter and decide what the reader knows about them and how this is known:

Main Character (hero)

AXEL

1. Axel is a young man who has lost his father, and feels very badly about the loss.

Page 2: *He squeezed his eyes tightly, forcing the tears to run, and could see again the wound the hole made in the churchyard and breathe the plowsmell of fresh soil.*

2. He doesn't have a good relationship with his mother, and dreads a future living with her, without his father.

Page 2: *Imagining for last two days what it would be like living alone with his mother, had left him in doubt that he could do it.*

3. He's in so much pain over the death of his father and his prospects for the future that he even feels suicidal.

Page 2: *. . . there was a force that pulled him down. He was drawn by the desperate ache of his wanting to be with his father, wherever that was, to follow him and be near him again.*

4. He has the ability to control his emotional reactions.

Page 3: *Axel hadn't cried for years, and he wouldn't allow himself to at the funeral.*

5. He has a good, long-time friendship with Molly, but not a romantic one.

Page 3: *Her fine hair against his lips and the warmth of her through their clothes felt good. He saw in his mind the delicate features of her light-skinned face framed by dark curls. They had not touched like this before, and it was a new feeling for both of them.*

6. He starts a romantic relationship with Molly.

Page 5:   *. . . .but now she looked different to him. More grown up. More like a woman. Not like his mother was a woman, but not like Molly was still a girl, either. He reached down and took her hand again and they walked that way.*

7. He, like most teenagers, is unsure of a way to express his feelings.

Page 6:   *"I'd like that, Molly. You're the only friend I've got. I mean. . .there's nobody else. Even if there was, I would. . .you—"*
          "I know what you mean, Axel. I feel the same way about you."

MOLLY

1. Molly is a young woman about Axel's age and is his long-time friend.

Page 5:   *Molly had been there, and it was the way it always had been, but now she looked different to him. More grown up. More like a woman.*

2. She is a sensitive and kind girl who cares for Axel in a romantic way.

Page 3:   *. . . saw the tears and reached up with the fingers of one hand and wiped them away. . .,*

Page 3:   *"I've been worried about you ever since your father got sick."* and *". . .Because, I really worry about what happens to you. You know that, don't you?"*

Page 6:   *"We're special friends now, aren't we, Axel?"*

AXEL'S MOTHER

1. Axel's mother doesn't have what we recognize as a good relationship with her son.

Page 2:   *Imagining for the last two days what it would be like living alone with his mother had left him in doubt that he could do it.*

2. She has begun to drink, or at least lately likes her ale very much.

Page 6:   *"I should be. She'll want her jug of ale. Probably she should have it tonight, too."*

TECHNIQUES OF TEACHING NOVELS

Now that you've studied the first chapter and know all this good stuff, what to do with it? It has to be used by you to help your students. Of course, you're going to show them how to understand it and apply their understanding to this and future novels.

A note on what doesn't help. There's no training that helps students when we ask them to tell us the story in their own words. This is just recall and doesn't teach them to think, only remember. We don't suggest that students read as a memory exercise, so what's the point of asking for recall?

To help you help your students, there are included invented conversations that show you ways that you can help your students apply their understanding of the techniques of literary examination. These might seem idealized to you. That's good, they are. It wouldn't help you at all to give you conversations that didn't work, would it?

Once students are shown how this process works and we ask them to apply it to books they have read, we can do two important things for them. One, we can help them apply their understanding of a technique of examination to a piece of reading they are familiar with; and two, we can walk them through this application. Below is a conversation between Bob, a 12 year-old boy, and his teacher. The point the teacher is trying to make in this short example is that authors make a conscious decision to create their main characters in such a way that their intended readers will identify with them. This is just an introduction of this training process. There'll be more on this later. This type of conversation could be had with more than one student, a whole roomful if desired. For simplicity in this example I've used one, Bob.

Bob:	I've finished the first chapter, now what?
Teacher:	Did you like it?
Bob:	Sure, it was okay.
Teacher:	Not too exciting for you?
Bob:	Not much happened. When do I get to the dragons?
Teacher:	The author has to set you up for them.
Bob:	What's that mean?
Teacher:	You won't like the fight with the dragons very much unless you've identified with the main character. And you haven't yet—enough anyway.
Bob:	I already know who the main character is.
Teacher:	I'm sure you do, but that's not the kind of identification I'm talking about.
Bob:	Huh?
Teacher:	I don't mean identification like with a picture on a driver's license.
Bob:	What do you mean?

Teacher:	I mean that the author has to create the character so that you would feel like him or want to be like him.
Bob:	How's that work?
Teacher:	Let's go back and look at the first chapter together and see what the author's doing to help you feel like or want to be like the main character.
Bob:	Sure, but I just read it and I don't want to be like that Axel at all.
Teacher:	I bet we could find some things that you and he have in common. If this is a well written book, and you're in the group that's the intended audience, we'll be able to find some stuff.
Bob:	I'm sure the intended audience, 'cause I like books about fighting or hunting or ones that have lots of action.
Teacher:	Let's look. You read until you come to something that you and this character might have in common.
Bob:	. . .I'm at the third paragraph and I don't see anything.
Teacher:	Go back with me to the first line and look at the first word. What's that tell you?
Bob:	The kid's name is Axel.
Teacher:	Okay. Now, what if it were Bob? Would you think you and he had anything in common?
Bob:	Of course I would.
Teacher:	What if it were Jack?
Bob:	Okay, what does that tell me?
Teacher:	What do the names Jack and Bob have in common?
Bob:	They're both common names.
Teacher:	What if the character's name were Running Bear?
Bob:	Okay, I see what you mean. We have names that are alike in that they're both American names.
Teacher:	Where do you suppose Running Bear would live?
Bob:	Boy, do you make this hard! Bob and Jack are both names that kids like me have. There're three kids in my group that are named Jack and not one named Running Bear.
Teacher:	Good. The author knew that he'd have a bigger audience (he'd sell more books), with a character named Axel than he would with one named Running Bear.
Bob:	There aren't any Axel's in my group either.
Teacher:	Okay, but you see the point, don't you?
Bob:	Sure, he gives the kid in the story a name that's in some way like the names of the kids who would read the book might have.
Teacher:	Good for you. Now, what do we know about where this Axel lives by reading the second sentence?
Bob:	He lives where they have grass in the spring.
Teacher:	Is that like where you live?

19

Bob: I see what you're doing. All the things that the author tells us about Axel are things that would be like things I might know something about.

Teacher: Sure, or something that you feel, or have done, or thought about. If the author can make you feel like the kid in the story, you'll like the story a lot more.

Bob: That makes sense.

Teacher: Now, if you feel like the kid and he gets eaten by a dragon, you'll be more likely to feel the teeth as they sink into your back.

Bob: Ouch! I see how that works.

Teacher: On the other hand, if an author were to make the main character someone you didn't like, maybe a dumb, spoiled, nasty boy, and he got eaten by a dragon, maybe you wouldn't care so much.

Bob: I think I might even root for the dragon.

Teacher: I think you understand how reader identification works now.

These conversations will continue in chapter two. You could have similar conversations with your students with each of the elements of fiction that are presented here.

Chapter 2

The Mother Of All Mothers

In which we are introduced to Axel's mother and get some understanding of their relationship. Axel's problem is made clearer to us.

Saddam Hussein introduced this phrase to the American people when he described the Gulf War tank battle that was about to take place as "The mother of all battles." Your students may not be aware of this second meaning—the largest, the meanest, the most expensive, the most impressive of anything is the mother of whatever it is.

LOCATION and TIME

The story takes place before there was electricity and in a village in a very remote location in some place other than the U.S.

Page 8:   . . .*and the lamplight behind her created a shining crown of her hair*. . .

Page 9:   . . .*smell the old ale and smoke from the fireplace and lanterns hung on the walls.*

CHARACTERS

AXEL

1. Axel, we find, does care for his mother. He would rather the men in the tavern think the ale is for him than his mother.

Page 9:   *Now they must think that the ale's for me, he thought. Well, that's all right, I don't mind. Better me than my mother. . .*

2. He is unsure about how to deal with unpleasant things when with adults.

Page 11:   *Axel didn't know what to say or what to do. Looking at the man, he waited for him to continue.*
             The man smiled and said, "It's spring."
             "Yes."

AXEL'S MOTHER

The reader has further evidence of Axel's mother's self-centeredness.

Page 8:   *"You had no call to go off for hours and leave me all by myself." She was blocking the doorway, and Axel knew he wouldn't get in the house until she had said what she wanted to.*
            "I'm sorry, Mother. I—"

Page 9:   *"The least you could do is get me a drink now that I need it so bad." She reached out and pushed her fingers against Axel's shoulder. "This hasn't been the best day of my life, you know. It's not every day that a new widow buries her man, now you think about that instead of that girl."*

Page 12:   *"You'll have to do all the things he did. It's that or we have to sell it and you can work for someone else. We'd have to move where there was someone for you to work for."*

Page 13:   *"You think you're going to take up with that tavern owner's girl, don't you? You think you'll just forget about your responsibilities, eh? Just go off somewhere and let your old mother starve?"*

Page 13:   *"It's not been easy for me this last year, you know. What with your father sick and in so much pain. There's been no one I could talk to about anything. It's seemed like I was all alone with the world coming down on top of me."*

Axel's mother doesn't say and do mother-like things. She doesn't talk about how hard the last year must have been for Axel or that she understands how much he must miss his father. She doesn't console him over his loss. His mother's attitude and actions contribute to the conflict Axel faces.

MINOR CHARACTERS

THE MEN OF GREENWATER

The adults that Axel must face, now that his father is dead, try and take advantage of his youth and inexperience. The following conversation might help you understand how to help your students see this.

Teacher: How do you see Axel being treated by the adults in his life?

Bob: Rotten.

Teacher: So what does *rotten* mean?

Bob: You know, not good.

Teacher: Can you give me examples of what you mean directly from the text?

Bob: Sure, Axel has a conversation with Molly when she saves him and he thinks that he's never had one like it before. And he should have had ones like it with his parents.

Teacher: Read me that section that tells you this.

Bob: *Axel had never had a conversation like this with anyone before. No one had ever asked him how he felt or if he would be all right. It was strange, but good.*

Teacher: Good. Any more?

Bob: Lots. Axel's mother doesn't think about how Axel feels about his father dying, just about herself.

Teacher: Read me that part, too.

Bob: *She reached out and pushed her fingers against Axel's shoulder. "This hasn't been the best day of my life, you know. It's not every day that a new widow buries her man. Now you think about that instead of that girl."*

Teacher: That makes her sound pretty cold, doesn't it?

Bob: Yes, and the men in the bar try to take advantage of him.

> *When Axel had walked to the table and was looking down at the men, the fat man looked into his eyes for long enough to make Axel feel uncomfortable and then said, "Last fall I talked to yer father and we agreed about his farm. He told me he'd sell it to me this spring."*
>
> *Axel didn't know what to say or what to do. Looking at the man, he waited for him to continue.*
>
> *The man smiled and said, "It's spring."*

"Yes."
"Yes, what?"

Teacher: It looks like all the man was doing was reminding Axel of what his father had done. How is that taking advantage of him?

Bob: He doesn't have to do it that way. He makes Axel nervous by looking at him and not saying anything. Lots of adults do that. And he talks to him about the farm just after his father dies. That's not a good time to do that.

Teacher: Of course, you're right. Good reading.

Bob: And he makes fun of Axel drinking ale.

> *"Ask yer mother if it's not so. And ya should do that before you drink all that ale." The other men laughed.* This goes on for almost the whole book.

Teacher: When does it stop?

Bob: I don't remember. Let me think. . .I know. When he becomes a knight and tells the king that he'll be a farmer. The other knights laugh at him. But, when the king says that he thinks it's a good idea, the knights stop laughing and no one makes fun of him again in the rest of the book.

Teacher: Why is that?

Bob: Because he's a man now.

Teacher: Don't men make fun of other men?

Bob: Not to their faces, and not all the time.

Teacher: Does this happen to you and your friends?

Bob: Sure, all the time. Not like it happens to Axel, but in a more subtle way.

CONFLICT

The conflict is introduced in chapter two. Axel will have to work. He won't have enough money to marry Molly. He'll have to live with and care for his mother. The nature of the conflict is established also at this point. It's man against society. Axel lives in such a place and time and under such circumstances that there's no way that he can assume the functions of a man, but he no longer can remain a child. He is between the two—he has to take care of his mother, he loves Molly and wants to continue his relationship with her, but he has no income or any way to earn enough money to do what he wants or must do. The elements of the conflict will be further developed in chapter three.

Page 11: *They might have to sell, and then what would they do? If his father had been planning on selling, what did he have in mind doing next? They were farmers. They would just have to buy more land somewhere else. The farm wasn't very big and they wouldn't get much for it. Sure not enough to buy a bigger place.*

Page 11: *If she wants to sell the farm, what will I do? I don't want to leave Greenwater and Molly. I can't do that. If mother sells, she'll have to move. There's nothing for her to do here. I'd have to go with her and take care of her, and I don't know how to do anything but farm. We'd have to work for someone else on their farm.*

Page 12: *Greenwater's so small there isn't anyone here we could work for except that rich, fat man. I don't want to spend the rest of my life working on someone else's farm. I'd never get to see Molly and I'd spend all my time with Mother.*

POINT OF VIEW

The point of view remains consistent. The narrative voice knows what Axel experiences and has the ability to be in his mind. It still doesn't have knowledge of what is in the minds of the other characters or what is happening out of Axel's presence.

EXPOSITION

The farm where Axel lives is small and they are just able to survive with it.

Page 11: *They were farmers. They would just have to buy more land somewhere else. The farm wasn't very big and they wouldn't get much for it.*

Chapter 3

How Dreams Get Born

In which we see Axel confront his problem. His ideas are not very wise or realistic, but he is young and optimistic about life.

CONFLICT

Axel is falling in love with Molly.

Page 17:   . . .*where Molly lived [was] at the far end of the village, and he could just see them. Looking at where she lived, worked—and slept, quickened his heartbeat.*

The reader learns that Axel's mother is not someone Axel will enjoy living with.

Page 22:   *But, now that Axel's father was gone, his mother centered her attention on him.*

In the few short weeks since the funeral and their walk home, he has discovered he is in love with Molly. This complicates the conflict, because, now that's he's in love, he has even more reason to want to function as an adult.

The conflict is fully established when Axel learns that Bobson has made some arrangement with Cedric's father to have Molly marry Cedric. Now Axel is under even more pressure. When he tells Bobson that he wants to marry Molly, he is ridiculed and is told about the promise of the trade of Molly to Cedric for help with the inn.

Page 25:   *"I've talked to your mother about what kind of a boy you are, and I sure don't want the likes of you for a son. No thanks, boy. Just forget that idea."*

Page 25:   *"Besides, Cedric's father and I've talked. Nothing set yet, but he talked about investing in the inn. It needs work and he has the money, and there's nothing better than keeping it in the family. So, just forget all about those silly ideas."*

Page 28:   *He would have to take Molly with him. And, Cedric was a problem now, too. How could Molly's father do that to her? Axel knew that she didn't think much of Cedric. But his family did have a lot of land. And Axel had no money. If they went away together, they both would starve. What he needed was a way to make money in a hurry. The problem was that there was almost nothing he could do that anyone would pay for.*

Bobson, in public, makes fun of Axel and his love for Molly. This sets the conflict. Axel is pitted against the rest of his world. He has no allies. His father is dead. His mother is drinking to escape the pain of her husband's death and is so self-centered she doesn't think of her son. The people in his town make fun of him. He has no education. There is no employment and no prospect of any. His love for Molly and his dream of a life with her are doomed by circumstance.

The author has spelled out the conflict in the following passage. This is about as clear a definition of the conflict as there could be. At the same time the conflict is defined, Axel's idea for the resolution of the conflict is first introduced. In very uneven conflicts, such as are found in adventure novels, the hero never has enough strength or resources to make it seem possible to overcome the opposing force. If the hero succeeds it is because of wit, skill, brains, or luck. Axel can't change his society. All he can do to win in this conflict is to be very lucky or skillful. In this case, to kill a dragon for the bounty.

Page 29: *Now, if me and Molly could get some money, but that's not about to happen. I do know of men who split up their farms and gave the pieces to their sons, but it can't be done for me. There's no way for me to make enough to live on, unless. . .unless I could get some money by. . . I don't know. By killing a dragon or something.*

In adventure novels, the elements in the conflict have to be unbalanced. The protagonisic force—the side of the conflict that wants something—has to be much weaker than the antogonistic force—the side that prevents the hero from succeeding. In this novel there is such an imbalance. All of his world is against the young hero and his desires.

If the reader identifies with Axel at this point in the novel, then the author has captured the reader and can hold the reader's interest throughout the conflict resolution.

SUB-PLOTS

One sub-plot—Axel's need to help his mother now that his father is dead, is established in this chapter.

Page 31: *He felt sorry for her and at the same time guilty that he wanted to get away, then remembered the little house that he wouldn't be able to see from his and Molly's farm.*

The reader learns of Bobson's deafness. This will play a part in the sub-plot concerning Axel's mother and how he resolves that conflict.

Page 26: *Sometimes Bobson couldn't hear what was said to him even if the person talking was right in front of him. He watched their lips, Axel noticed, when people spoke to him.*

INCITING FORCE

Bobson makes fun of Axel. Axel's learning of Bobson's plan to marry Molly off to Cedric, and Axel's mother's plan to have him work for someone else drive Axel to desperation.

Molly confirms to Axel that Bobson has a plan to marry her off to Cedric. This is the final push.

Page 32:   *"I'm going to get enough money so we can get married."*
             Molly leaned back and said, "Well. Nobody told me anything about this. My father's talking about me marrying Cedric late this summer. Besides, who said I could marry you?"

Page 27:   *"This boy wants to take over my bar. He thinks I'll let him take both my Molly and my inn. I had to set him straight last week."*

He now must face the opposing force, no matter how strong it is.

Page 30:   *I'm going to do it! I don't know how, but if some men can make a fortune, I should be able to.*

Chapter 4

All Losers Have Stories To Tell

In which Axel meets for the first time people outside of his village and encounters what he sees as adult wisdom.

This is the first of the references to sports and sport expressions. This is something that coaches say when a member of a team makes an excuse for losing.

CONFLICT

Axel is full of optimism and hope. He is naive in attitude and belief. The reader is shown this by Axel's view of his adventure when he wakes up and talks to a squirrel.

Page 35:   *Axel thought, Here I am, one of the last great dragon hunters, being driven off from my first home away from home by a squirrel. If I leave here, it'll think it chased me away. He opened his other eye.*

Axel shows the reader that in his hope and innocence he has a sense of humor about his conflict resolution.

Page 36:   *As he tied his long, blonde hair back with a piece of twine, he looked up into the branches and called out, "You beat me this time, beast, but down this road somewhere your big cousin is waiting for me, and I'll put up a better fight then."*

Axel is introduced to characters who are not from his village. People who don't know him. They give him what is called conventional wisdom—the common person's understanding of anything. Axel, in his innocence, doesn't know that these two people he meets in the small house at the side of the road don't know anything about dragons. He believes what they tell him. This shows the reader that he is still looking at the world as a boy might. This is a much different way to see things than the way he sees things at the end of the novel.

Page 41:   *"Yah, gold and other things," and the man swung his large, round head toward Axel. "Tell em, Mother."*
Axel asked, "Do you know about dragons?"
The old woman squinted her eyes and looked into the far corner of the room. "When I were a girl there was dragons. That were a long time ago. . .when I were younger. But I remember it clear. Sometimes it don't seem like that long ago, but I know is were true. I know that to be a fact."

Axel is naive and he believes what the old woman and her strange son tell him about dragons.

Page 45:   *Axel started the third day of his adventure. He now knew a lot more about dragons than he had learned in all of his previous sixteen years.*

Chapter 5

Pre-Game Analysis

Another sports reference. On television, the sports announcers many times have an analysis of the coming contest. They talk about the problems the teams and players have had in their past games and might experience in the game just about to start.

Axel learns some information that he feels will help him in his fight with dragons. Chapter 4 and this chapter are meant to do two things. They introduce Axel to the effects of encounters with dragons and personal experiences with them; and are designed to increase the suspense. Chapter 5 reinforces what Axel learns from the old woman—that dragons are nasty and very dangerous. This builds up the power of the symbol that the dragon has become—the problems connected with becoming a man.

Chapter 6

A Wizard At His Game

In which Axel meets an old man who says he is a wizard. He helps Axel to understand how powerful dragons are and helps him find a way to fight them.

Your students will be happy to tell you about the wizardry of Magic Johnson, Michael Jordan or the golfer, Tiger Woods. These men really are wizards at what they do, and the reference in the sub-title for chapter six is to both the game this man may be playing and his ability at it.

Axel has been drifting with a very vague plan. He obviously doesn't know enough to kill a dragon. What he needs to help him be successful is education or training. He can't kill a dragon with his strength or skill and luck is very chancy. (Yes, I intended that.) His meeting with Sidney is designed to give him that education. This will greatly enhance his chances of success.

CHARACTER

SIDNEY

Sidney claims he's a wizard. The ambiguity of this is intentional. He may not be a wizard, only call himself one. If you give your students the job of proving that he is or is not a wizard—they must do it with examples and quotations from the text—they should have a good time with it.

There are suggestions that Sidney knows about Axel and his plan to kill dragons from talking to the three men that Axel meets in the mountains. They not only direct Axel to seek out Sidney, but they are headed that way themselves.

Page 51: *They hadn't gotten to his valley yet, just heard about him. Len said, "I wouldn't go over there where no wizard was if it was just me alone. Ya can't trust 'em. They trick ya."*

Page 51:   *The three men had started off much earlier than Axel wanted to, and they seemed to be in some hurry. Just before they walked back down the side of the mountain, they had pointed in the direction of the valley where the wizard lived.*

It's possible that they offer Sidney information that he can use to earn some money. They're certainly looking for an opportunity to earn some themselves. This could account for Sidney's knowing Axel's name and what he wants. On the other hand, there is very little text evidence that the men tell Sidney about Axel. There is some evidence, however, that they've been to Sidney's valley.

Page 53:   *A slight movement at the edge of the far tree line caught his attention. Axel shielded his eyes from the sun and examined the valley. Three dark figures faded into the shadows of the distant trees and then were gone.*

If Sidney's a fake, and he has learned about Axel from the three men, then he is faking his lisping. He then probably is faking the shifts in time. There is some evidence of fakery.

Page 57:   *Looking at Axel, almost as if he were making sure he was being seen doing it, he held an egg in his hand for a moment as if warming it, blew onto his closed fingers, and slid it under the blanket.*

Page 60:   *He pulled back the blanket on the bed, picked up an egg and began to peel it. . .*

The suggestion here is that Sidney uses magic to hard-boil an egg by blowing on it. Notice that he makes sure Axel sees what he's doing. Suspicious action for a wizard. Then we have Axel discovering a raw egg in the same blanket.

Page 61:   *Axel sat on the bed. He felt and heard what sounded to him like an egg breaking. He put his hand under the blanket, and when he pulled it out it was covered with raw egg. As he wiped his hand on his cloak, he watched Sidney carefully.*

There is even a suggestion here that Axel is beginning to doubt Sidney.

Here's an indication of Sidney faking that your students may not catch. Sidney tells Axel that he can't say his esses because his donkey ate the ess from a set of letters he was using to cast a spell. This would mean that any word that has an ess in it would have to be pronounced with some other sound—like a *th* sound. But Sidney uses the *th* sound for the *s* sound in some of the words he speaks, even if the sound isn't produced by the letter *s*. For instance, he uses *exthpect* for the word *expect*. Since there is no letter *s* in *expect*, Sidney should be able to say it correctly. But he puts *th* in it. He must be doing that consciously. Thus faking it.

It doesn't really matter much to Axel, whether Sidney's a fake or not. Axel learns enough from his sessions with Sidney to increase his chances of success. He develops a plan for killing dragons.

Teacher: I would like you to take a piece of paper and draw a line down the middle of it from the top to the bottom. On the left of the line, make the heading: Wizard. On the right side of the line, make the heading: Fake. Now list in the left side all the reasons you can find in the text to support the idea that Sidney is a real wizard. List on the right side all the reasons you can find to show that Sidney is a fake wizard.

Bob: What will that do for us?

Teacher: Good question. You should always think that question even if you don't always ask it.

Bob: What about an answer?

Teacher: Another good question. Always ask for information you feel you need.

Bob: Well?

Teacher: Well what?

Bob: What good will the lists do us?

Teacher: They'll show both of us how you've come to the decision you have about Sidney.

Bob: How will they do that?

Teacher: When you have the lists, you'll see that there's much more support for one side than there is for the other. This will help you understand why you feel about him as you do.

SUB PLOTS

Sidney and Axel become friends. Sidney encourages Axel to try something less dangerous to get money. He is worried about him. Axel recognizes that Sidney can't work like he used to and also is very poor and needs to live with people who will care for him.

Axel would like to stay longer with Sidney, and Sidney would welcome it.

Page 66: *Axel took much longer carving the letter than he had to and wasn't sure the wizard wasn't taking longer to teach him about dragons than was necessary.*

There is some suggestion that Axel feels for Sidney. We later learn, in the scene with the king, that this is true.

Page 78:   *Sidney turned and looked into Axel's eyes and said very clearly, "You could stay here if you want to," and he lifted one hand, then let it drop. "I could teach you how to be a wizard."*

Axel shook his head and said, "I'd really like to stay here with you, Sidney, but I've got things that I've got to do."

"I know you do, my boy. It was just a thought. . .I get lonesome sometimes."

"I'm sorry. But I can't. I'd. . .like to," Axel shrugged, "stay, but—"

"I understand, Axel. You have to go."

Axel waited for a long moment, then was surprised that his voice was high and squeaky. . .

EXPOSITION

Just as does Axel, we learn a good deal about dragons in this chapter. The romantic nature of Axel's quest is reinforced by his belief that he can burn up dragons.

Page 70:   *Axel was shouting, "I found It! I can kill dragons. I know how to do it. Sidney, light the lamp. Let me tell you what I figured out."*

A realistic look at what Axel plans to do would encourage us to take out life insurance on him. But this is fantasy, and for him this works.

CHARACTER IDENTIFICATION

Continuation of the chapter-one conversation about identification,
but this time with a roomful of students

Teacher: Now that you all understand the process of reader identification with the main character, does anyone see in the second chapter what you think the author put there for that reason?

Jan: What are you asking for?

Teacher: I want to know if anyone recognizes anything the author's done in the second chapter for the purpose of reader identification.

Leon: Like what?

Jan: I know what you mean. He makes Axel look like a kind person.

Teacher: Why do you say that?

Jan: He says that it's better that the people in town think the ale is for him than for his mother. That's a nice thing for him to do.

Teacher: Do you see that, Leon?

Leon: Sure, I do. . . Now.

Teacher: Good. Do you like him better because the author shows his kindness?

Phil: Sure, I do.

Ralph: Yah, but if his mother drinks the ale, she should take the rap for it.

Teacher: What's that mean, Ralph? How should she take the rap?

Ralph: Axel should tell the men in town that he doesn't drink the ale, but his mother does. She should admit it.

Leon: Hey, Ralph. Would you like Axel better if he ratted out his mom?

Ralph: If she drinks the drink, she should take the stink.

Jan: But this isn't real life. This is a book.

Teacher: What difference does that make, Jan?

Jan: We're supposed to like Axel, and in real life we're not *supposed* to like anybody.

Teacher: Ralph, do you understand what Jan's saying.

Ralph: No, what's she saying?

Teacher: Jan, say that another way, can you?

Jan: It's like, in real life there's nobody making us like anybody, but it's not that way in a book. In a book the author's trying to make us like the character.

Ralph: But I don't like the mother if she puts her drinking off on her kid.

Teacher: But, what does that make you feel about Axel.

Ralph: He's a chump for letting it happen.

Jan: But, he's being kind.

Phil: I know. He's taking the blame so his mother doesn't have to. He's being kind to his mother. I think he's a good guy 'cause he does that.

Tom: That's the way we're supposed to think.

Teacher: How do you know that, Tom?

Tom: 'Cause you told us that's what the author's trying to do.

Teacher: Okay, Do you think that the author knew you'd feel that way?

Tom: He probably did. He'd think that I would like him more if he was kind than if he was mean to his mom.

Teacher: Does anyone else see anything here that would make a reader like Axel?

Sam: There's adults that take advantage of Axel, and he doesn't seem to be able to do anything about it.

Teacher: Like who?

Sam: Bobson makes fun of him. The fat farmer makes him stand there while he stares at him. He asks Axel questions he can't answer and embarrasses him when he can't.

Teacher: Does that help you identify with him?

Sam: Sure.

Teacher: Why?

Sam: Kids are always being taken advantage of by adults.

Teacher: Even you?

Sam: All kids. And there's nothing any of us can do about it.
Teacher: Give me an example from your life.
Sam: When adults talk to us, like in school, and they're really boring, we have to listen to them, and we can't tell them to be quiet. Adults say that to kids all the time, but we can't say things like that to adults.
Teacher: That doesn't happen to Axel, though.
Sam: No, but that's an example of how I'm taken advantage by adults. That's why it helps me identify with Axel. I think the author knew that about kids and knew we'd identify with him because of it.
Teacher: You think adults say that to you for their good and not yours?
Sam: That's what I think.

It's hard sometimes to resist clearing up misunderstandings that some students have about why adults do some of the things we do. But at this time this teacher is trying to get the students to think clearly about the identification process in this book. That's the important function of this discussion. I imagine this teacher would make a note about what Sam has said and at some other time come back to it and help him think through what's going on in his mind about the relationship between adults and kids.

Teacher: You see anything else you think the author did for that purpose?
Alice: I know. Axel worries about what will happen to him. All kids do that. Maybe not in the same way Axel does, you know about farms and his mother and all, but we worry about other things. Stuff we don't have any control over, just like Axel.
Teacher: That's good thinking. You have the idea about character identification. You're going to run into more later in the book that will strengthen your identification.
Phil: Why so much?
Teacher: The more you identify with Axel, the more you'll pull for him when he has to fight the dragon. If you don't like him or want to be like him, when he gets in trouble and is about to die, you won't care.

It'll take some practice working together before you and your students can have conversations like this one. But, it will happen if you ask open-ended questions and not give them the feeling that you're looking for someone to say the right word or words. Ask them what they think and then respect what they say.

Chapter 7

There's Lots To Learn From Failure

In which Axel meets a man who has fought with a dragon and been beaten by it. He receives some good advice.

CHARACTERS

WOUNDED WARRIOR

The wounded warrior contributes to the story in a number of ways: 1) He adds to the suspense by making it obvious that Axel hasn't a chance against a dragon; 2) His fight puts a dragon in the area; 3) It places the dragon in a specific location. Up to this time the dragon might or might not be out there somewhere. Now the reader knows that a dragon actually exists, where it is and what it's like.

The knight has been defeated.

Page 82:   *"Where was the battle?"*
The man's voice was still hoarse but much stronger now. "On the side of a mountain." There was a slight smile on his face. "I lost."

A dragon is put within Axel's reach.

Page 85:   *"Go back home, boy. Tightly's dragon lives near the top of that mountain," he said, pointing north toward the tall, snow-covered peak. "Even if you could climb to its lair, you would be killed."*

A trained fighter is defeated by the very dragon Axel must face.

Page 85:   *The man was quiet for a moment, then turned and looked at Axel, "That's what I was doing all day yesterday." He dragged himself into his saddle, and with much pain on his face, sat upright. "I can tell you this much, you won't stand a chance. Dragons are smart and mean. And very tough. You'll just get killed. Go back home while you still can."*

AXEL

Axel doesn't seem to understand that there is great danger facing a dragon. He romanticizes his fight with it.

Page 82:   *In front of him is the long, curving line of the enemy. The sun glints off their weapons, and their banners snap and dance in the wind. There is a stillness in the air as before a storm. He sits tall upon his horse, and then with his knees, urges it slowly forward. He can hear his men behind him murmur in admiration. He can even hear their thoughts, "He's going out alone to do battle with the best they have. What a leader."*

There is a stirring in the line before him—a nervousness in their ranks when they realize who approaches them. He can hear them whispering, "It's Axel. Axel is coming. Who can we put up against Axel?"

EXPOSITION

We learn from a person who has had direct contact in a fight with a dragon what Axel must face.

Page 85:   *"I can tell you this much, you won't stand a chance. Dragons are smart and mean. And very tough. You'll just get killed. Go back home while you still can." He looked at Winthton, then turned back to Axel again. "And take the donkey with you."*

Chapter 8

The Practice And The Prize

In which Axel practices his skill, meets a representative of the temple and learns of a prize for killing the town's dragon.

CHARACTERS

AXEL

Axel is still the same naive boy in chapter eight that he is in the first few chapters. He still daydreams and talks to himself and animals. There also is some small indication that he is beginning to take seriously the job of killing a dragon. He remains focused on his romantic quest for riches (manhood).

Axel talks to Winthton and plays at being a warrior.

Page 87: *"Now, Winthton, it probably won't ever be necessary for me to use this sword at all, but I have to have it with me, and I have to look as if I know how to use it. We can't let anyone know how we plan on killing the dragons. If anyone finds out how we kill dragons, then they could do it too, and we can't have that. If this works like I think it will, we'll be the only ones who can kill dragons and get away without being killed or wounded. So, you have to be careful that you don't give us away."*

Page 88: *"They have to think I cut and hack them to death. Or—whatever warriors do."*
The practice with the sword Axel viewed as a kind of play acting.

Axel doesn't know whether his fire idea will work, but he imagines it will, and he talks himself into thinking he'll be successful. This is the thinking of an immature person facing great danger. Not too untypical for young men even today. Think of young men driving fast. Very dangerous, but they all think nothing bad will happen.

Page 89: *The first time he hit the bag with an arrow with the point on it, his mind raced with excitement. The flame goes down the dragon's throat, the ugly beast roars and there's a look of shock and pain as it begins to burn inside. It had been standing on its hind feet with its tail thrashing behind it. It had been leaning down sucking in air. I hold my aim until just the right moment, then release the arrow. The point sinks into the roof of the open mouth. The burning rags, soaked in oil and tied around the shaft then lit just before firing, continue to burn as the dragon takes in more air. The flame disappears down the green throat and the scales covering the belly of the beast begin to glow. The dragon's eyes get big, and it screams in pain. It lies down on its side and smolders. To hide how I killed it, I slide the sword from its scabbard and plunge it into the still beating heart. I'll have the bloody sword as evidence.*

Even if Axel plays and dreams, he does take seriously his job of killing a dragon. I think he's been convinced that it's dangerous work.

Page 88:   *The practice with the sword Axel viewed as a kind of play acting. He accepted it as a show, but the work with his bow he took very seriously. He spent at least two hours a day practicing. He could hit his target almost every time from thirty paces.*

He had constructed a dragon's head from a bag of rags.

There is the first indication that Axel is at all worried, or that he is even thinking about what the dragon is doing or might be able to do.

Page 90:   *He wondered if the dragon was up there watching the town and the approaches waiting for him. Can it see me? Of course not. I'm too far away. But, once I start the climb, the dragon will know I'm coming and be waiting for me.*

THE TAILOR

Axel is introduced to the aggression of commerce and its lack of interest in people except as a way to make money.

Page 91:   *He passed a tailor's shop. When the tailor saw Axel stop, he must have recognized him as a stranger, for he hurried out and seized him by the arm. "That's an old outfit, and I know you to be a young man interested in style. I can tell by the intelligent look on your face. Come and let me show you some new material that just came in. You'll like it." He pulled Axel's arm toward the shop.*

Digging his boots in the ground, Axel refused to be moved. "I have no money to buy clothes. I do have a question—"

"Some other time then, boy." The tailor turned quickly and re-entered his shop.

THE PRIEST AT TIGHTLY

For your discussions, you shouldn't identify the religious figures as priests in any particular religion that your students might be familiar with. This is a fantasy, and Christianity or any other religion is not represented in it. There are and have been priests in all religions in the past, and so these priests depicted here need not be offensive to anyone. They might even be Druids.

The priest first offers to help Axel.

Page 93:   *"Yes, my son. What is it you wish to know? Are you lost?"*

As soon as the priest learns that Axel might be important to him, he changes. First he performs his office rituals. Then he talks to Axel in ritualistic ways.

Page 93:   *"You killed the dragon?" he hissed with surprise.*
             "No, I plan on doing that."
             The priest took a thong from around his neck and ran its knotted length through his fingers. Fastened to it, cut from a dark wood, was a figure that Axel couldn't make out.

When the priest realizes that he may have to deal with Axel, he speaks in his professional jargon, much as lawyers, doctors, teachers and politicians do. You might point out to your students that this priest does this every time he is confronted with his duty.

Page 94:   *"My son, have nothing to do with Evil. Have nothing to do with the Evil's dragon. Have nothing to do with those who do." A fine rain of spittle fell on Axel's face, and when he didn't respond, the priest leaned closer until their noses were almost touching. "Touch not the Evil. Touch not those who touch the Evil. Touch not those who touch those who touch the Evil."*

The priest is not too bashful to ask for the gold (a donation to the temple), and he tells Axel that if he gives the gold away, he will save himself. We see through this, but Axel doesn't.

Page 94:   *"Who—Who will give me gold?"*
             The priest turned and looked to the far end of the street, then whispered wetly into Axel's face, "The blacksmith's son. He will give you gold to kill the Evil's helper. Save yourself. Give the gold to me."

HAMMER

Page 95   *"After I kill the dragon I"ll buy that one," he pointed, "the one on the right I think."*
             The laugh started deep in the large man's chest. It rumbled like summer thunder and burst from his mouth in waves. He kept his eyes on Axel, but he threw back his head and was thoroughly enjoying himself.

Hammer does what many people of limited intelligence do—he makes fun of others so that he can feel superior. He laughs in this scene, not because there is anything funny, but because he wants to make Axel seem even dumber than he is himself.

Page 96:   *"I have come to kill the dragon. I was told you have a reward for this. Have I come to the right place?" Hammer was now laughing so hard that he had to sit down and was holding one hand against his side and was supporting himself with the other one.*

Page 98:   *"You can sleep in the back on the straw if you want."*
Hammer laughed again, "With the chickens, eh, Dragon fighter?"

THE BLACKSMITH

The blacksmith represents the people in society who take advantage of others, not because they may gain anything material, but because they can get the favor of authority figures. The world is full of people who function this way. You could list a dozen from your experience as could your students from theirs. The blacksmith knows what the trick with the egg is and goes along with it, even though he knows he won't benefit from it.

Page 97:   *Reaching under a chicken, he pulled out a large brown egg. He held it between his fingers in the light coming from the front of the shop and said, "We will balance gold coins against an egg. The coins will equal the weight of the egg. You must prove to us that you have killed the dragon to collect. The town elders have made this arrangement. I've been selected as the one to pay the reward when the dragon's dead. The priest is keeping the gold."*

Your students might have a good time talking about whether or not the blacksmith knew what kind of an egg the priest was going to use to determine the amount of the reward.

POINT OF VIEW

It might be good to have your students again examine the point of view to establish that it remains constant.

SUB-PLOT

Axel is involved in a sub-plot with the priest. We are given a foreshadowing of a problem with Axel's reward payment. Your students should expect that this problem will be returned to before the end of the book and that Axel will get all that he has been promised or that he will lose the conflict in this sub-plot.

Chapter 9

When First Meeting A Dragon. . .

In which Axel first fights a dragon.

METAPHOR

The four fights with the dragons serve as Axel's fight to gain manhood, and so they become an extended metaphor. This mountain that Axel must climb can also serve as a metaphor for the reaching he must do to gain acceptance into adult society. Notice the descriptions of the cliffs and ledges. There is even reference to larger beings.

Page 100: *The mountainside was a series of ledges and cliffs—like stairs made by giants.*

In his desire to be a man, his goal is clear. In his quest for gold (adulthood) he can see where he must go, and that the path will not be easy

Page 100: *On the third ledge was the dark, shaded entrance of the dragon's lair. His head tilted sharply back, Axel counted the ledges as he looked for an easy way up.*

When he is home and thinking about what he wants to do, he can see the faults and problems of the adults in his world but cannot see how they could help him get what he wants.

Page 100: *There was none [easy way up]. The vertical slabs were not entirely smooth, as there were breaks in their stone faces, but none that he could see that would make the climb easy or even safe.*

Page 100: *There was no way he was going to get the dragon to come down to him. He had to go to it.* This is a metaphor for the problem Axel has in the beginning of the book. Axel has a desire to talk with his father and ask his advice. He cannot have that and realizes that if he ever gets what he wants he must go to it. It will not come to him where he is.

Page 100: *Looking at where he would have to go, he wished that he had had a chance to talk longer with the wounded man about his climb. There was nothing he could do about that now. There was no way he was going to get the dragon to come down to him. He had to go to it. He slung his bow over his back as he walked up the path to the first riser of the stepped precipice.*

CHARACTERS

The dragons are certainly characters in this story. They are the physical manifestations of the tough, uncaring, and many times, ugly aspects of the adults in Axel's world. The dragons notice Axel when he confronts them and is a problem for them. They want to use or devour him. Your students might have fun comparing the characteristics of the dragons with the characteristics of the adults Axel has contact with.

Teacher: Do you see any characteristics that the dragons have that are like any of the characteristics the people in Axel's world have?

Bob: What do you mean?

Teacher: If the dragons are symbols of the problems Axel must solve to become an adult, then there should be some similarities between the dragons and the problems.

Bob: Like what?

Teacher: Okay, here's one. The dragons are seen by Axel as being very powerful. If the dragons are symbols, then Axel must see some of the people in his society as powerful. Does he?

Bob: I see what you mean. Sure, Bobson is seen as powerful.

Teacher: How?

Bob: He's Molly's father. He can control her. He even offers her to Cedric's father in exchange for money for his inn. He would have to be powerful to do that in Axel's eyes.

Teacher: Do you see that trade to be a good thing?

Bob: No, it's not right to trade people for money.

Teacher: What would Axel say about that kind of a trade?

Bob: That it was wrong.

Teacher: Is there anything in the book about what Axel sees about the dragons that might be like that trade?

Bob: I see what you're getting at. Sure, Axel sees the Dragon as evil.

Teacher: Read me that part.

Bob: Page 105: *Never has there been a more evil creature, Axel thought.*

Teacher: Any other sections that suggest that the dragon is evil?

Bob: The priests calls it evil.

Teacher: Where?

Bob: Page 94: *"My son, have nothing to do with Evil. Have nothing to do with Evil's dragon. Have nothing to do with those who do." A fine rain of spittle fell on Axel's face, and when he didn't respond, the priest leaned closer until their noses were almost touching. "Touch not the Evil. Touch not those who touch the Evil. Touch not those who touch those who touch the Evil."*

Teacher: Good for you. Do you see any other similarities?

Bob: Sure, the dragon is seen as powerful.

Teacher: Okay, what is there in Axel's life, other than dragons, that is a powerful force that he must fight?

Bob: He must obey his mother. He's got no money and can't earn any. And he has to have money to marry Molly. Cedric's father's rich and plans on getting Molly for Cedric. There's lots of similarities.

IDENTIFICATION

Axel is shown in this chapter to be persistent, brave, determined, resourceful, agile, clever, and smart. These are all characteristics that the young reader would appreciate and want to emulate. Of course, Axel must be all of these things to survive. This is after all a fantasy novel.

SUSPENSE

As in most fantasy novels, there is a good bit of suspense in this story, and your students should be aware of how they have been manipulated by the author. Your students should know that suspense is an emotional reaction on the part of the reader and is not something that is put in stories by writers. Writers can create what we call a suspenseful situation but cannot write suspense. This must be produced by the person appreciating the situation. So, in order for writers to create suspense, they must be able to control the readers' emotions throughout their stories.

The writers who want to engender an emotional reaction, which must be accomplished in fiction, have two jobs. Though related, they are accomplished by different methods. They must determine the emotional condition of their readers at each step in their stories, and they must control the emotional changes of their readers to the events in their stories.

Although there are other steps involved in the creating of this reaction of a feeling of suspense in their readers, there are some basic things authors must do. They must:

1. Fix the time and place to create the mood they need
2. Create a character with whom their readers can identify
3. Foreshadow a threat to this character

4. Make the force against the character much stronger than the character
5. Put the character and the threatening force in direct confrontation
6. Put the character in a life threatening or very dangerous situation
7. Delay the resolution of the conflict a number of times

The resolution can go either way. This doesn't affect the suspense. The author attempts to create the feelings of suspense in the readers of this story by following these steps:

1. **Time and Place**:

   Suspense/adventure stories are essentially romantic, and it adds to the suspense/romance to have the action take place in some indefinite past time and in an unfamiliar, foreign or romantic place.

   This story takes place in the past. The exact time is not known, but it is understood to not be a real past because there are dragons in it.

   The place of the action, as in many fantasy novels, is in an area that we might associate with England. This is the traditional place for fantasy stories of knights, castles, and dragons.

2. **Creation of Character**:

   The three methods of creating a character with whom the reader can identify have been listed earlier, but it is essential that your students understand this process. Only when this happens can the reader feel empathy when the character comes into conflict with the superior force.

   If there is no identification process, then, when the character gets into difficulty, the reader will not care and there will be no suspense.

   The intended readership for this novel is intelligent young people between the ages of ten and fifteen years.

3. **Foreshadowed Threat to Character**:

   There are many indications that Axel faces a threat to his dreams of manhood—where he would be able to make a life for himself and do what he wants.

   Page 9:   *I know you been with that girl from the tavern. Just 'cause your father's dead, you think you can do anything you want. Well, you can't.*

Page 11:   *Axel didn't know if the man was telling the truth or not. If his father had agreed to sell the farm, he hadn't told him, and he didn't know what his mother would want to do. If that were true, then he and his mother might have to honor that promise. They might have to sell, and then what would they do?*

Page 11:   *He was sure that he and his mother would have to make some decisions now. If she wants to sell the farm, what will I do? I don't want to leave Greenwater and Molly. I can't do that. If mother sells, she'll have to move. There's nothing for her to do here. I'd have to go with her and take care of her, and I don't know how to do anything but farm. We'd have to work for someone else on their farm.*

Page 12:   *"You're going to have to do your father's work now. This farm's so small that it was just big enough to let us live. You'll have to do all the things he did. It's that or we have to sell it and you can work for someone else. We'd have to move where there was someone for you to work for."*

Page 13:   *"Do I have to decide now? Tonight?"*
            "I figured you'd want to put it off. You think you're going to take up with that tavern owner's girl, don't you? You think you'll just forget about your responsibilities, eh? Just go off somewhere and let your old mother starve?"

Page 21:   *She turned back to her bowl and said, "I don't know what we'll do now that my husband's gone. There's so much work and the boy can't do it all. What do you think I should do, Good Farmer John?"*

4. **Strong Opposing Force**:

If the forces against the hero in suspense are not greater than the reader might think the character could handle, the reader would not worry about the character solving the problem, and there would be no suspense. To help establish this feeling in the reader, the force against this character is made to be much stronger than the character.

You might have your students identify the forces in conflict in books they have read and describe the differences in the relative strengths of the forces.

There doesn't seem to be much of a chance for Axel, and the young reader, having identified with Axel, surely will empathize with him. When the reader realizes the forces against Axel, there will be feelings of suspense: "Is it possible for Axel to succeed against these odds?"

The forces against Axel are two-fold. The main conflict in the story, of course, is Axel against the forces of society which seem to conspire against him and his desires for adulthood. The symbolic, or metaphoric force against him is the power and skill of the dragons. These opposing forces should be very easy for your students to identify.

The main forces that oppose Axel and his goal are economic and social. He needs to have money to marry Molly and have the kind of life he wants. He has no money and no prospects of getting any. He is opposed by the farmers and their greed, by his youth and inexperience, by Molly's father, Bobson, by his mother and her demands and her need to drink, by the smallness of their farm, by Cedric and his family money, and by his lack of education and skill.

The symbolic forces that oppose Axel, the dragons, are much larger and stronger than he is. They easily defeat trained knights. They are smart and tricky. Axel has poor fighting skills and almost no weapons. Axel is young and slight of build. He appears to stand no chance of living past an encounter with a dragon.

Your students might benefit from listing the characteristics of these two forces. They should be able to identify clearly the strengths of the society that Axel must fight and the strengths of the dragons. They might enjoy discussing these same forces that they recognize in their society.

5. **The Conflict:**

The conflict is clear in both the main struggle and the symbolic one. Axel against the forces of the social structure and Axel against the forces of nature—in the form of the dragons. Man against society, man against great odds. Axel faces a challenge—he must make enough money to marry Molly before the summer is over, for at that time Molly will have to marry Cedric. If he doesn't do this he will be forced to live with his mother on their small farm and watch the girl he loves marry someone else. He will be trapped by his social and economic position.

6. **Resolution Delayed**:

It is during the delaying of the resolution that the suspense is experienced and most keenly felt by the reader. If Axel were to discover that he loves Molly and he were to inherit enough money from his father to marry her, there would be no suspense in this story. Just as there would be no suspense if he were to kill each of the dragons quickly and easily.

The suspense is built in the main conflict by Axel's desire for adulthood being thwarted by social pressures and in the symbolic conflicts by his close calls with death in his fights with the dragons.

Chapter 10

Even Before There Was Small Print

In which Axel earns the gold and is given a good lesson in trust.

SUB-PLOTS

One of the institutions that Axel has conflicts with is the temple and its priests. These men are portrayed as greedy and tricky. This situation produces one of the steps in his becoming an adult—learning to deal with such adults.

The first priest speaks to Axel in a sing-song of ritual. He has warnings in groups of three.

Page 93:   *Almost in a singing way, the priest said, "The temple does not have a dragon. The dragon is an agent of Evil. I know not of a dragon, I am a man of the gods." He turned to go.*

After the priest learns that Axel is planning on killing the dragon, the priest wants to take advantage of him by asking for the reward.

Page 94:   *The priest held him with his eyes and the crooked fingers of one hand. "Talk not of the Evil. Listen not to those who would talk to you of the Evil. Seek not those who would tell you of those who have talked to the Evil. Give me the gold."*

The priest and the blacksmith have a plan to cheat the young dragon slayer out of the reward. Axel is in conflict with both priests as they try to cheat him. The first priest with the type of egg used to weigh the gold against. The second with the placement of the bag of gold. These small conflicts must be resolved in Axel's favor.

In the first conflict Axel is cheated but later beats the priest at his game by using the priest's own words. This is a clear indication that Axel is learning to function in the adult world.

Axel is cheated by the first priest:

Page 97:   *Reaching under a chicken, he pulled out a large brown egg. He held it between his fingers in the light coming from the front of the shop and said, "We will balance gold coins against an egg. The coins will equal the weight of the egg."*

Page 119:   *The priest spoke sharply, "No. I have chosen the egg. We will balance the gold with an egg I choose. That is the way it is done in this town, and it is what the people in this town want."*
               Axel turned to face the priest and said, "That seems fair to me. I trust you."

Page 121:   *Axel couldn't believe what was happening. When the blacksmith had told him about the reward, he had been holding a chicken's egg. Axel had been sure that was what they would use to balance against the gold. This looks like a songbird's egg, a thrush maybe, he thought.*

At this point in the development of Axel as an adult, he is still innocent enough to deny that the priest has cheated him.

Page 122:   *He [Axel] had kept his part of the bargain, and the priest did what he had said he would. So he hadn't really been cheated. And a priest wouldn't do that. He wasn't sure what had happened, but he knew that things hadn't turned out the way he expected they would.*

In chapter 17 Axel gets the best of the priest. Your students should be able to pick out the page(s) that are the climax point for the conflict in this sub-plot.

Page 226:   *"Do you remember what you told me about the selection of the second egg for a second dragon?"*

Page 228:   *The priest pulled the figure from Axel's hand, stepped back and faced the crowd. "If there were a second dragon, I would pay the reward myself. With my own gold."*
               "And I would be able to select the egg used to balance the gold?" Axel could tell the priest was suspicious now, but he had to continue, he was trapped.
               The old man nodded and said, "You could select the egg."

Page 234:   *The priest hesitated again, then said, "All right, that's what I said. You can pick the egg. I don't see what the fuss is all about; all eggs are about the same," and he smiled.*

(I see this as the climax point in this sub-plot. Your students might have a different view of this.)

48

Axel stepped down to where Winthton was and took the sling from his back. He placed it on the first step of the temple and looked up at the priest. "Send someone for a large scale."

Page 234:   *Axel unwrapped the dragon's egg and put it on one side of the butcher's scale. That side of the balance arm dropped hard to the stone of the step, and Axel looked at the priest.*

The second priest tries to cheat Axel:

Page 132:   *The priest urged Axel to follow him, and he led him and the men to the platform. He pointed to a small leather bag on one side of the altar. "On this side we have the temple's holy stones. Special stones selected by the temple and blessed by me to give good fortune and to keep away evil."*

Page 132:   *The priest chuckled, "The safest place in the world." He pointed to the other side of the altar. The men moved that way. "That is where we keep the gold for the reward."*

Page 135:   *Axel watched him and said to himself, I must not make a mistake this time. Let's see, the town will give me the bag on the left. I was facing the altar when the priest said that, so the bag with the gold must be the one on my left.*

Axel has learned about adult behavior to be suspicious of the priest and checks up on him:

Page 137:   *Axel watched carefully as the priest knelt and took a few of the small gold coins from the bag on one side of the altar and placed them carefully in the other bag. Then he switched bags! Now the bag with the gold is on the right side when a person is facing the altar. The other bag on the left has the holy stones in it with a few gold coins on top of them. Strange.*

Axel prevents the second priest from cheating him:

Page 148:   *Axel stepped to the left of the altar, to the bag that now held just a few coins covering the holy stones. He held it up so the people could see it. "I have earned this gold." The people stopped moving toward the door and turned to face him. "I have also earned the right to spend it as I wish."*

Page 148:   *Axel reached into the bag and took out the few gold coins that he had seen the priest put there the night before. These he handed to the priest and said to him. "Be kind enough to use these few coins to help the people who have been driven off by the dragon." The people cheered. Axel then handed the bag to the priest. "I wish to buy a whole bag of stones. I will trade this bag of gold for one bag of stones."*

Page 148:   *". . . If ordinary holy stones are good enough for you, then they are good enough for me," and he crossed to the right side of the altar and picked up the bag of gold he had seen the priest put there in the night. He held it up for the crowd to see.*

Your students should recognize that Axel is much better able to deal with adults on his return trip. He has been successful in this respect in his rites of passage into manhood.

Chapters 11-15

In which Axel kills his second dragon. He meets the king and kills the third dragon, though he is wounded in the fight. He meets a beautiful girl, Marie.

Chapter 16

Party Time

In which the king celebrates the killing of the kingdom's last dragon. Axel is made a knight and is given the king's horse and a knight's sword. He is now officially a man.

CLIMAX

There is a point in all conflicts where, because of something that happens, it becomes apparent who the winners of the struggles will be. At this point one side must win and the other side must lose. There is still conflict, but the forces that will win are identifiable. This force in adventure stories is usually the protagonistic force.

Axel has been searching for a way to make enough money to be able to marry Molly. He has traveled to distant places, sought information, traded his skills for training and killed dragons. This puts him much closer to his goal, but he needs a formal confirmation of his new position as a man and an adult. He has this when the king makes him a knight.

Page 216:   *"I will give you the highest honor I can. You are now a knight in my kingdom. Rise, Sir Axel."*

From this point on, Axel is a member of the adult society in his world. You might have your students list the differences in the ways Axel talks, acts, and treats others now that he's an adult. Have them work with Axel's dealings with: the priests, his mother, Bobson, Sidney, the warrior on the road by the side of the river, and the people in the town of Tightly.

Axel now has the trappings of manhood. He has a beautiful horse, a large amount of gold, a heavy, new sword, and fine clothes. These things do not make him a man, but they do give him the appearance of one.

Your students might find it interesting to discuss manhood in terms of their society. You might ask them to define the difference between masculinity and manhood. They might be surprised at the difference between what girls and boys think on this subject.

Your students should be able to list the actions, objects, and attitudes that demonstrate when a person in their society has reached adulthood.

Notice the difference in the way Axel speaks just before he recognizes that he has his adult status and just after. The boldly printed section is the climax of this novel. This is the point at which Axel realizes he has reached manhood.

Page 216:   *Axel felt foolish talking about his plans with the king in front of all the knights. When he spoke, his voice was so soft he could hardly hear himself, "I. . . We talked about buying . . . there's a farm. . ."* **I'm now a knight. The king has just made me one, and I'll act like one.** *Axel straightened his back and looked his king in the eyes. His voice was clear and loud enough for all those near the king's tent to hear and understand, "I will be a farmer. Molly and I will be married, and we will farm as much land as I can afford to buy."*

It is much more common in plays to have such an obvious climax to the conflict, but your students should be familiar with its recognition in fiction, also.

Even though he now sees himself as a man, Axel is still vulnerable to the pain of embarrassment.

Page 217:   *The king's laugh rolled out over the fairgrounds. The knights laughed with him. Axel felt as if he had been kicked in the chest. He could hardly breathe and looked at his feet. Tears pushed behind his eyes and his throat closed tightly.*

Chapter 17

Return Match

In which Axel returns to Tightly and wins the reward he should have been paid for killing the first dragon.

CHARACTERS

Notice the similarities between Axel's first meeting with a warrior by the river near Tightly and his second meeting with a different warrior. The positions of the two men are reversed. In the first meeting, Axel asks the questions, and in the second meeting, the warrior asks them.

In the first meeting the knight has been in a battle with a dragon and warns Axel off. In the second meeting Axel has been in battles with dragons and he warns the warrior off. These differences are a result of Axel attaining adulthood.

In the first meeting Axel asks the questions.

Page 85:   *Axel took hold of the reins near the bit and led the man's horse up to the path, asking questions the whole time. "How did you come to fight the dragon?. . . Where did you find it?. . . How did you plan to get the reward? . . .Did you kill it?. . . Wound it?. . . Did it burn you? Please tell me."*

In the second meeting the warrior asks the questions.

Page 221:   *Jeffrey mounted easily and sat tall on his horse. "Can you direct me to a town that might have had dragon trouble lately?"*

In the first meeting the warrior asks Axel if he wants advice.

Page 84:   *"Would you like some advice, boy?"*

When Axel says that he would like advice, the warrior says:

Page 84:   *"Go back home and work in the bar with your Molly."*

In the second meeting Axel offers advice to the warrior.

Page 221:   *"I can give you some good advice if you want it."*

Page 222:   *". . .Even if there were dragons, you wouldn't be able to succeed with your sword or even a lance. You would need. . .," he paused and tried to think of a way to say what this man needed to hear, "to see a man like Sidney."*

These two encounters demonstrate that the problems Axel has are not unique to him. They are common. They even transcend generations. In the last chapter Axel meets a young boy who wants to be just like him. The boy now faces the same problems that Axel has earlier. He wants to solve them in the same manner that Axel has.

Your readers should recognize that Axel and the boy are very similar and that the boy now faces the problem that Axel faces in the early chapters.

Page 261:   *When Axel turned toward the inn, he noticed a tall but slender boy who had edged up to him and stood there quietly. Axel almost bumped into him.*

Page 261:   *The boy looked down at his feet for a moment, then into Axel's face. "Someday I want to be just like you. If there aren't any dragons left, how can I do that?"*

Axel gives the boy the best advice he can. He tells him to seek knowledge, and that that will help him become a man. He points toward Sidney as an example of where knowledge might be found.

Page 261:   *Sidney was tying the bag with the egg in it onto Charger's saddle. Axel motioned toward his friend, and said to the boy, "Ask a man like that one. One who knows a great deal about . . .what you need . . . and other things. One who will help you when your time comes."*

THE DRAGONS

The dragons, as a metaphor for the problems that Axel faces reaching manhood, become extinct with Axel's killing of the last four (except, maybe, for the egg Axel finds). This would eliminate the possibility of any other boys being able to attain manhood in the same way Axel has.

With Sidney's suggestion of it being a double-yoked egg (twins), the possibility of their use for future transition into manhood for boys is assured.

Page *260*:

> *He opened his eyes and looked at it with wonder and said very softly, "And I think one on this side; there may be two." He was looking at it carefully and running his hand over its smooth surface, feeling of it with great tenderness. "We'll just have to wait and see."*
>
> *Axel leaned toward the egg, touched the green and gray surface and said, "Two what?"*
>
> *Sidney jerked away and said, "Never mind, Axel. I'll take good care of them. . .er, it."*

Chapter 18

The Program

In which Axel returns to Sidney's valley and invites him to his wedding.

Plot and Sub-plot

The author has to get Axel back home again to satisfy the resolution demands of the major conflict. If we were to call the conflict *Young boy against the confining and limiting aspects of his society*, then we would expect the character to return to his home town after becoming a man and function as an adult. He would have to be able to afford a wife, buy a farm, and demand and receive respect from the people in his town. This then would complete the conflict resolution, and this is exactly what happens in this and the last two chapters.

Chapter 19

The Perfect Match

In which Axel and Molly solve some of the sub-plot problems created by their plans to get married and live in Sidney's valley.

There are a number of sub-plot conflicts that are not yet resolved. They might be seen as 1) Axel's conflict with his obligation for his mother's needs for security; 2) His desire and ability to marry Molly; 3) His relationship with Bobson and the other men in the village; 4) His obligation to the king about finding him a wizard; 5) Bobson's promise to Cedric to trade Molly for help with his inn; and 6) His feelings of guilt over having killed the last dragon in the kingdom. Your students should expect these sub-plot conflicts, along with the major conflict, to be resolved in these last two chapters.

It might be a good idea for you to discuss these sub-plot structures with your students. They should be able to talk about the forces, conflicts and resolutions.

The resolution of the major conflict begins with the description of Axel's entry into his village.

Page 242:   *Axel felt he had been gone for a long time. Greenwater looked small to him. After all, he had stayed in the king's castle for a short time. He was more traveled than most of the people who had ever lived here. He was a rich and famous man. A dragon slayer.*

Axel is reunited with Molly.

Page 244:   *Bobson started to speak when Molly came into the room from the back of the bar. She cried out, "Axel. I knew you'd come back." She ran to him and threw her arms around his neck and hung on tightly.*
Bobson yelled, "Here now, we'll have none of that. Molly. . .stop it."
Axel and Molly saw nothing and heard nothing but each other. Both were talking. Both were listening. Staring into each other's eyes. In love. Together.

The author sets the reader up for the resolution of Axel's conflict with Bobson and the people in the village.

Page 245:   *Bobson was frowning. "That's no way to carry on in here, Molly. What if Cedric walks in? Think about what that would mean to me and the inn. And, what would the good folks in the village say?"*

Axel now has the respect of Bobson and the farmers.

Page 245:   *Axel had to explain his trip. The two farmers and Bobson wouldn't be put off. He was anxious to be alone with Molly, but Bobson said she couldn't leave the bar until he had told them all about the dragons. He wasn't anxious to talk about that part of it, but they insisted. That brought up the king. And then he had to tell about what the king had given him. Bobson's attitude changed toward Axel as soon as he heard about him being knighted. Now there was no charge for the drinks. It looked like the start of a party.*

The conflict between Axel and Cedric is now resolved.

Page 246   *Axel turned to look for Sidney and bumped into Cedric. Axel said, "Sorry I bumped into you, Cedric, it's pretty crowded in here." Cedric grabbed the front of Axel's shirt and pushed him against the bar. Axel looked into Cedric's eyes and said, "This is no way for grown men to behave, is it?" Cedric's growl started deep in his throat. Bobson saw the movement and reached over the bar and grabbed Cedric by his collar and dragged him to the back of the room telling him to quit bothering his important customers. Bobson followed him out the back door and Axel didn't see him again.*

Cedric is finished off, and any question about Molly wanting to marry Axel is resolved.

Page 246:   *Molly told Axel how lonely she had been and he kissed her. They would be married as soon as he could bring the priest to Greenwater from the next town. What about Cedric and Bobson's agreement with his father? Molly said that she could take care of Cedric, and that he wouldn't be a problem.*

The conflict Axel has with his obligation to his mother is resolved at the same time that there is a final resolution to the problem Molly has with her father wanting to trade her off for help for the inn. The reader isn't told what these resolutions are yet, but they are revealed in the next chapter.

Page 247:   *"If there was just some way we could work it so my mother and your father didn't have to be alone, we could get married and not have a thing to worry about. But, I can't think of anyone who could stand my mother. She talks all the time and is so crabby. She would drive almost anyone crazy." Axel had a small twitch of a smile on his lips that Molly noticed.*

Molly began to grin and came back quickly with, "My father has problems, too. He was so mean to you when you asked him if you could marry me, I'll never forgive him. And besides, he's getting old, and his hearing is getting so bad, most of what's said to him he just doesn't hear at all." She smiled up at Axel. "I have to shout right at him now for him to hear me."

Axel looked at Molly.

Molly looked at Axel.

They both laughed. Of course. Perfect!

The author reveals the plan that Axel and Molly have for convincing their parents that their problems can be solved. Axel leads his mother's thinking to the point where she discovers a solution for her future. Clever boy that he is, he helps his mother come to the conclusion that she doesn't want to live with Molly and him on their new farm.

Page 249:   *"You can come to live on the farm near us if you want to."*

His mother was wide awake now. "What farm? Axel, what are you talking about? Make sense."

"I don't know any other way to say it, Mother. Molly and I are moving, and you can come with us if you want to."

Axel's mother was frowning deeply now, "Come with you where?"

"To a really nice valley about five days east of here. There isn't a town anywhere near it. It's in the mountains. You'd really like it. There wouldn't be anybody else around to bother you. No town or nosy neighbors at all. Molly and I have talked about it, and we decided you would like to have a little place all your own." Axel gestured with his hands, as he said, "We could build you one at one end of the valley and we could live at the other end."

"What?"

"Doesn't that sound nice, Mother?"

She stood up from the table. Her long dress caught under one of the legs of her chair and she ripped it loose. "Do you mean to tell me that you expect me to live way up in the mountains and never see anyone? Not on your life you don't. I'll stay right here."

Page 249:   *Her voice rose. "You can't just leave me here all alone." She was pacing back and forth in front of her son now, wringing her hands.*

Axel looked closely at his mother as he said, "Bobson was saying almost the same thing this evening about when Molly leaves. He'll be very lonely, too." He looked at his mother's face. Nothing happened to it for a short time, then he could see that she was getting an idea.

She lifted her hands and pushed her hair back from the front of her head. "He is a fine man, but I don't have too much to—" She squinted in the dim light and said, "What will he do for help when Molly leaves?"

57

Axel helps his mother convince herself that she doesn't want to live in the valley with her son.

> *"I was able to save quite a bit. I might even be able to give some to you to help Bobson fix up the inn, if things work out the way he wants them to. You know what I mean?" He smiled at her.*
>
> *She lifted her chin and pushed back her shoulders, and said, "I might not move to that valley with you and Molly. I always said I never would be a burden on my child, and I never will be. I can plan my own future. I don't really need you now, and I won't need you then. How much did you have in mind to give me to fix up the inn?"*

The reader is led to believe that Molly has a similar conversation with her father, Bobson.

Page 252   *Axel went to his bed that night thinking things might work out well for everyone. He wondered how Molly had done in her talk with her father.*

When Axel realizes that he has killed the only dragons left in the kingdom, he feels sad and guilty. The following passage sets up a conflict for Axel—his desire to kill dragons and his feelings of guilt when he kills the last ones.

Page 211:   *The air left Axel's lungs. He couldn't breathe. He had not realized that that was what it meant—his killing of the small female dragon, until the king said that. He looked at King Willard and asked, "The last one?"*
"Yes, my boy. There are no more, and there never will be any more. What a wonderful thing you have accomplished," and he patted Axel on the back. Axel's face had lost its expression. "That was. . .the last one. . .in all the kingdom? And I. . .killed it?" Axel stood.
The king also stood, and now looked down at him. "You don't seem excited, Axel. What is the problem? Are you still surprised that you could do it?"
Axel turned and looked in the direction he had traveled to kill the dragon. "Couldn't there be more somewhere else? Isn't it possible?"

The resolution to this conflict begins when Axel finds that the egg is still alive.

Page 252:   *Before blowing out the lamp, Axel brought his pack into the house. Putting it carefully on his bed, he took out the egg, sat with it in his lap and examined it closely. It felt slightly warm to him when he ran his hands over its dry, leathery surface. He thought again of its mother's cries. . . . She must have known it was the last one ever.*
As he was putting it back in his pack, he was sure he felt the surface move. A slight pressure on the palm of his hand.

Chapter 20

Post-summer Wrap Up

In which the problem Axel has with his guilt over killing the last dragon is resolved as Sidney finds that there may be two dragons in the egg. Axel helps a young boy understand that there is still hope for boys to find ways to gain manhood.

Page 260:   *Later that afternoon, when Sidney was talking about heading back to his valley, Axel gave him the egg. "Sidney, this is the last dragon's egg there will ever be and last night I think I felt movement inside."*

Sidney looked into Axel's eyes for a long time, then took the egg and pressed it to his ear. He stood that way for a bit, then said, "If so, we should be able to hear or feel. . . Yes! I think so." He turned it over and over, pressing his hands gently on it, then held it to his other ear. He shut his eyes, then squinted them together as he pressed it hard against the side of his head. He opened his eyes and looked at Axel and said, "And I think one on this side. Axel there may be two." He was looking at it carefully and running his hand over its smooth surface, feeling of it with great tenderness. "We'll just have to wait and see."

Axel leaned toward the egg, touched its green and gray surface and asked, "Two what?"

Sidney jerked away and said, "Never mind, Axel. I'll take good care of them. . .er, it."

Axel is accepted by his village as a man and a hero.

Page 253:   *When the men, who had to stand outside near the road because of the crowd already in the tavern, saw Axel and his mother turn the bend and head into the village, they let out a loud cheer. This brought out the people from inside the tavern. They all surged out to meet the new hero and his mother.*

Axel and Molly find the resolution to the problem about what to do about the needs their parents have. The perfect solution is to pair them off. The man who needs help with the bar and inn who is deaf, and the woman who talks all the time and needs a place to live.

Page 258:   *"Axel is a good boy. That's the way I raised him and that's the way he turned out. I'm sure glad he and Molly are going to get married. She's such a nice girl. I've been telling him for years that he should take an interest in her. She comes from such a good family. It's important for the better families to stick*

59

together. Don't you think so?" Bobson was smiling at her with a blank look on his face. She said, "Don't you agree with me?"

"Oh, yes," Bobson said, "It looks like it'll be a fine day."

She spoke loudly, "Did you talk to Axel yet about fixing up the inn?"

Bobson smiled and nodded, "You're right. I never had so much trade at this time of day before."

She continued, "We should talk about it. I always say that most things can be worked out. It isn't as if he doesn't have the money to help you out. After all, if he's going to marry Molly, it'll still be in the same family." She turned and looked for Axel. "Don't you think so?"

Bobson was filling a mug, "What?"

"I asked you if you didn't think so."

"Oh, yes indeed. Fine boy. Make Molly a good husband. Wants to farm I hear."

With the marriage, Axel's conflict with his society is finally resolved at the same time that the resolution of the problems with Bobson and his inn and with Axel's mother's future are complete.

Page 260:   *The ceremony was held in front of the inn. The sun shone brightly on the young people, the crowd drank and ate and enjoyed the short service. Bobson and Axel's mother stood side by side and looked very proud.*

What happens to Sidney and his need for a place to feel useful and his need for help because of his age is resolved with his decision to live with King Willard.

Page 261:   *Sidney was pleased. He smiled hugely and ran his hand down Charger's neck and said, "Thank you, my boy. If you ever need him, you can find us at the castle."*

The major conflict is resolved for Axel. But, on a larger scale, there is the same continuing conflict for all the boys of Axel's world. This is first introduced on:

Page 29:   *Now, if me and Molly could get some money. There's men who split up their farms and gave the pieces to their sons, but it can't be done for me. There's no way for me to make enough to live on, unless. . .unless I could get some money by. . . I don't know. By killing a dragon or something.*

The author tells the reader that Axel's story is just an example of this problem. We recognize how much Axel has changed when we see a young boy ask how he might become a man like Axel is now.

Page 261:   *When Axel turned toward the inn he almost bumped into a tall, slender boy who had edged up to him and was standing there quietly. He waited for the boy to speak, and when he didn't, Axel asked, "What is it, boy?"*

This greater conflict is resolved at the very end of the story. Axel, now a man, is asked by a boy who faces the same problem that Axel faces at the start of the story.

Page 261:   *It must have taken courage for the boy to talk to this knight, the new hero and dragon killer, but he looked up and, pushing his hair away from his face, said, "Sir Axel, are there any dragons left alive? My father said you killed the last one. Is that true?"*
       Axel looked over at Sidney who still had the egg in his hands but was putting it into the bag of rags. Turning back to the boy, he asked, "Why do you want to know about dragons?"
       The boy looked down at his feet for a moment, then back into Axel's face. "Someday I want to be just like you. If there aren't any dragons left, how can I do that?"

Axel tells the reader that there is still help for young boys in their reach for manhood.

Page 261:   *Sidney was tying the bag with the egg in it onto Charger's saddle. Axel motioned toward his friend and said to the boy, "Ask a man like that one. One who knows a great deal about . . . what you need. . . and other things. One who will help you when your time comes."*

THEMES

Deciding on the theme of a book is a very complicated process and there is no one answer. Good literature can be understood and enjoyed on a number of levels. I have had instructors tell me what the themes of books are, but I never could see the books that way. What a reader receives from a reading is particular to that reader's background, age, intelligence, and education.

You couldn't expect your students to understand a book in the same way that you do, just as you couldn't expect them to enjoy it in just the same way that you do.

There's a good question concerning whether the theme is even in the book. Instead, it may reside in the reader. It would be very hard to get good authors to tell what they feel are the themes in the books they've written.

It should help you and your students if you examine this book as if it were good literature. We know it's not, but we can pretend and use it as an exercise in understanding this form of art.

Because the theme(s) is/are determined by the reader(s), there is not one correct theme, but the following ways of looking at this book will suggest to your students some possibilities.

1. This novel can be understood, appreciated, or examined for theme based on it being an adventure. This is the least complicated way to look at it. *Dragonslaying is for Dreamers* then becomes a story about a young boy who seeks adventure killing dragons. Adventure is certainly something many seek, and this then is a legitimate way to examine this story and it would produce an acceptable theme.

2. This novel can be considered by looking at it as a satire of the institutions that society has created. This is not nearly as clear a way to look at this story as are some other ways, but it does work as a way to generate theme. A young boy seeks success in life and is thwarted by the institutions that ostensibly have been created to help him: parents, adults in the form of community members, religion and its leaders, educational experiences, neighbors, parents of friends, and the natural forces that provide for us all. Axel must seek his own solutions and provide for himself against not only these people as they represent their institutions, but against wild beasts that would eat him. He finds the solutions for his problems by seeking the help and advice of an outcast member of that society. One who is neither respected or liked. The irony of this situation should be evident and appreciated by your students.

3. This novel can be understood as an examination of the rites of passage. A young boy wants to become a man, but there are no established paths to ease his way. This involves the readers translating the experiences that Axel has into the experiences that they would be familiar with.

4. This book can be seen as an allegory—a story that has a moral that is demonstrated by symbolism or abstraction. If this is done, we would have a fictional situation designed to teach or illustrate a moral principle. A number of them might be obvious to your students:

   - *If people are good, good will come to them.*
   - *Innocence, virtue and a just goal will win any contest.*
   - *Persistence and courage in the face of great odds make any quest possible.*
   - *Knowledge and skill applied with determination can win against fear and greed.*
   - *To survive and prosper, one must learn all that is possible and work hard.*
   - *Belief in yourself is as important as a belief in others.*
   - *Any goal is possible to attain if faith is strong enough.*

- *Even when successful, it is important to be generous and kind.*

5. This novel can be appreciated as an examination of the existential positions we all find ourselves in as we confront problems in our lives. If this story is looked at this way, we have a young man who must make decisions about his life. His future is determined by what he decides to do. He is not a pawn of society, rather an engineer of his own experiences, but he must accept the responsibility for his decisions.

It might be very important for your students to understand that the literature they experience can be a personal relationship between the skill and imagination of the authors and themselves. They must be the ones who determine how they will benefit from the reading.

Authors may not give us truth in their fiction, but good literature gives us ways to deal with and understand the joys and problems we face.

INDEX